A Professionals' Guide to 24 Urban Self-Defence and Close Quarter Combat Systems

Compiled by Robin Barratt with...

ADAM PARSONS, AL CASE, ARIS MAKRIS, BENJI CHURCHILL BRIAN FAY, CYNTHIA MORRISON, DAVID KAHN, JONATHAN HODGSON, KEVIN O'HAGAN, MO TEAGUE, NICK MAISON, NORM WILLIS, PAUL 'ROCK' HIGGINS, PETER ELLIS, RUSSELL JARMESTY, SIMON MORRELL, STEVEN TIMPERLEY, STEVE TAPPIN, TONY SOMERS, TYRREL FRANCIS, YURI KOSTROV, VIRGIL O. CAVADA

Published by Robin Barratt
ISBN: 978-1542831697
Text © Robin Barratt 2017 and all the authors herein.
Images © Robin Barratt and the photographers herein.

All rights reserved. No part of this publication may be reproduced,
distributed, or transmitted in any form or by any means,
including photocopying, recording, or other electronic or mechanical methods,
without the prior written permission of the publisher,
except in the case of brief quotations embodied in critical reviews and
certain other non-commercial uses permitted by copyright law.
For permission requests, email the publisher at the address below.

W: **www.robinbarratt.co.uk/books/combat/**
E: Robin@RobinBarratt.co.uk
E: RobinBarratt@yahoo.com

About Robin Barratt

A former doorman, CPO and trainer of CPOs, Robin has been writing and publishing since the year 2000, after stepping away from full-time security operations and training; an industry he was in for almost twenty years previously.

He is a genre best-selling author of six non-fiction true crime books, one biography, three self-help guides as well as two travel and one poem anthology about Bahrain where he lived for four years, and where he was also commissioned to produce and publish a quality book for one of the biggest Arab merchant families in the Gulf region.

He also compile and publish a poetry and short prose book collection featuring writers and poets around the world (*Collections of Poetry and Prose*), and has written and published a number of Kindle ebooks on a diverse range of topics and subjects.

On top of this, he founded and published *Tough Talk*, an acclaimed online magazine interviewing martial artists, boxers, combat specialists etc., founded *The Circuit* magazine for the British Bodyguard Association, founded *On The Doors*, the UK's No1 magazine for Door Supervisors, and published the *International Directory of Security & Close Protection*.

He has also written a number of articles for magazines and newspapers worldwide including *Gulf Insider, Sur La Terre, Time Out, Norfolk magazine, Absolute Lifestyle, Signature, Exotic Car magazine, T Qatar (New York Times* style magazine) and many others.

Other Titles by Robin Barratt

TRUE CRIME / REFERENCE
Doing The Doors
Confessions of a Doorman
Bouncers & Bodyguards
Respect and Reputation (with prisoner Charlie Bronson)
Mammoth Book of Hard Bastards
Britain's Toughest Women
How To Find Work as a Close Protection Specialist
On The Doors - online magazine
Door Girls – OUT SUMMER 2017

TRAVEL
My Beautiful Bahrain
More of My Beautiful Bahrain
Poetic Bahrain

POETRY & SHORT PROSE
HAPPY - A Collection of Poetry and Prose on Happiness and Being Happy
WAR - A Collection of Poetry and Prose on the Bravery and Horror of War
TRAVEL - A Collection of Poetry and Prose on Travels and Travelling
LOVE - A Collection of Poetry and Prose on Loving and Being in Love
LONELY - A Collection of Poetry and Prose on Loneliness and Being Alone

COMPLEMENTARY THERAPY
A Professionals' Guide to 30 Holistic, Healing and Complementary Therapies

And others....

Go to:

www.RobinBarratt.co.uk

www.facebook.com/Robin-Barratt1

www.Amazon.co.uk/Robin-Barratt/e/B0034PY84C

Contents by Subject...

CONTRIBUTORS
Page 8

INTRODUCTION
By Robin Barratt. Page 18

AGNI KEMPO - Surviving Real-Life Combat
By Yuri Kostrov. Page 22

APPLIED ESKRIMA – Developing the Reflex Speed of the Student
By Virgil Cavada. Page 29

AWARENESS RESPONSE DELIVERY (ARD) - As Street Related as Realistically Possible
By Adam Parsons. Page 36

BARTITSU - A Fighting Style for Gentleman
By the UKBA. Page 39

COMBAT JU-JUTSU... From the Battlefields to the Streets
By Kevin O'Hagan. Page 43

CONCEPT MARTIAL ARTS - An Idea, or a Way with No Way
By Brian Fay. Page 47

ETIQUETTE CLOSE QUARTER COMBAT & CONTROL - Anything Considered, Everything Measured
By Benji Churchill. Page 56

ESCRIMA CONCEPTS - A Weapon to Unarmed System
By Steve Tappin. Page 64

FIGHT FORTRESS - Keeping it Simple and Effective
By Simon Morrell. Page 71

HARD TARGET COMBAT SYSTEM - Practical Approaches to Aggressive Engagements
By Mo Teague. Page 78

ISRAELI KRAV MAGA - Globally Recognized for its Simplicity and Brutal Efficiency
By David Kahn. Page 83

JEET KUNE DO - The Way of the Intercepting Fist
By Norm Willis. Page 93

KARATE – As a Self-Defence System
By Tyrrel Francis. Page 97

KNIVES & EDGED WEAPONS AWARENESS PROGRAMME (KEWAP) - Pragmatic, Time-Friendly and Highly Effective
By Steven Timperley. Page 102

KWON BUP - A Study in How a Martial Art Dies... and is Resurrected
By Al Case. Page 108

MEANSTREETS SELF-DEFENCE SYSTEM - Raw, Brutal and it Works
By Russell Jarmesty. Page 115

MUAY THAI – As a Self-Defence System
By Tyrrel Francis. Page 125

PANKRATION - The Grandfather of all Martial Arts
By Aris Makris. Page 130

PROGRESSIVE KENPO - An Advanced Form of Traditional Kempo
By Jonathan Hodgson. Page 134

REAL COMBAT SYSTEM - An Efficient and Tough Fighting System
By Tony Somers. Page 144

SPHERE COMBAT SYSTEM - Based Around Natural Responses to Action Under Stress
By Peter Ellis. Page 150

STAGE COMBAT - From Karado to Kong
By Cynthia Morrison. Page 153

TOTAL KRAV MAGA - A Dynamic and Practical Combat System
By Nick Maison. Page 158

V.I.P.A. TACTICAL TRAINING SYSTEM - Embracing Change, Evolvement and Open Mindedness
By Paul 'Rock' Higgins. Page 165

Contributors...

ADAM PARSONS – ARD & Bartitsu. Pages 36 & 39
The United Kingdom Bartitsu Alliance (UKBA) was set up by Adam Parsons in 2015. Bringing together martial artists from a variety of backgrounds, the UKBA seeks to continue and expand the recognition and legitimisation of the Victorian martial art of Bartitsu, in its historical context, as both a competition sport and combat art. Also to promote both groups and individuals who seek to advance their knowledge and level of participation; to help promote and inform to the general public of the history of Bartitsu, its part in the development of martial arts in the UK and its place as a bona fide style in the martial arts world, and to actively seek the instructors of each modernised form of Bartitsu who are willing to uphold the knowledge and traditions of the art. UKBA is not currently seeking to be an Association, a Federation or a Governing Body but it is in fact a friendly and welcoming networking organisation for practitioners. Please remember, the UKBA strongly encourages its Affiliates to retain and in fact expand their affiliations with a wide range of organisations in the martial arts and self-defence world upon registration. The UKBA is open to all regardless experience within the art. The UKBA does not promote the petty politics that many other groups seem to contain, there are no hidden agendas, and it will not interfere with its valued Affiliates' practices either, all affiliates are open to practice and instruct their classes as they wish, there is no need to sign up to a 'right way' of doing things, and so on.
W: www.UKBartitsu.com

AL CASE - Kwon Bup. Page 108
Al Case walked into his first martial arts school, Chinese Kenpo Karate, in 1967. He eventually became an instructor and wrote the training manual for the school. In 1969, Under Robert J. Babich, Al began studying Kang Duk Won, which included the art of Kwon Bup. Mr. Babich, before mastering the Kang Duk Won, had studied with Don Buck, and crossed-fists with Mas Oyama. Upon achieving his black belt in the Kang Duk Won, Al began studying such arts as Wing Chun, Shaolin Gung Fu, Tai Chi Chuan, and Pa Kua Chang. In 1981 he began writing articles for the martial arts magazines, and had his own column in *Inside Karate*. Eventually, Al began writing books, and then putting his arts to video. This lead to his discoveries of Matrixing Technology, which is the first actual study of the martial arts as a science. Matrixing led to forays into a more spiritual realm, and these studies are described in his books on Neutronics. Currently, Al is the webmaster of *MonsterMartialArts.com*. He has written over 2,000,000

words on the martial arts, which makes him arguably the most prolific martial arts writer of all time. His works include not just the martial arts, but philosophy, poetry, many novels, children's books, mathematics, and even a book on *Pig Latin*.
W www.AlCaseBooks.com
W: www. MonsterMartialArts.com

ARIS MAKRIS - Pankration. Page 130

A son of Greek immigrant parents, Aris was raised in Park-Ex, one of Montreal's poor yet toughest neighbourhoods. Like many others of his generation, he was inspired by Bruce Lee and the martial arts boom of the '70s. He began his training very early in his life, but didn't get serious until he was in his late teens; he went from Japanese karate dojos to Chinese kung-fu schools, and everything else he could get his hands on that would answer the questions he had about martial arts and fighting. The streets he grew up in were tough and everyone was practising some form of combat art. Aris was a first generation Greek and in those days, and like any other multicultural city in North America, it was a time of clashes between cultures, and Aris often had one fight on his way to school, another in school and one on his way home. And that was only a warm-up for what was to come later in the evening when neighbouring gangs would meet and battle it out. Aris soon found out that learning the traditional arts wasn't helping him much in handling the reality of fighting efficiently, and his teachers did not have the answers either as they were basing their experiences on traditional martial arts movements which were not effective on the streets. Aris ventured into other combat arts like boxing and judo and, going from one academy to another, continuously sought out the toughest combat schools in the city. By the time he left school he was heavily bitten by the martial arts bug. Given his Greek academic upbringing, his culture's history, added to his ego-driven ambition to live up to his ancestors, and being of Spartan blood only fuelled the fire. It was in his late teens when Aris was told by one of his karate instructors about how Mas Oyama praised the Greeks for having introduced Pankration to the ancient world. Pankration was fully functional and complete martial art that catered to the warrior and in which proficiency in all areas of combat were attained; his ancestors from Sparta had exactly what he was looking for and the stage was set for his direction in life. In his late 20s he joined the Greek military and started teaching Pankration to military personnel. In 2006 he was inducted in the Martial Arts Hall Of Fame for the first time, made a number of documentaries for the History Channel, and quickly became recognized as the world's foremost authority on the Ancient Greek art of Pankration.
W: www.pankrationcanada.com

BENJI CHURCHILL - Etiquette Close Quarter Combat & Control. Page 56
Benji is the owner of Etiquette Security & Training UK, which has its own system of close quarter combat and self-defence, aimed at those working in the close protection and security industries, an arena in which there is often real danger. Having a traditional background in Hapkido and Taiho Jutsu, holding black belts in both, for the past twelve years Benji has been mastering the 'new age' approach to the science of combat and cross-training in styles such as Muay Thai, WW2 Combatives and traditional Ju-jutsu, allowing for just right mix of skills to create an effective close quarter combat defence system.
W: www.etiquettesecurityandtraining.co.uk

BRIAN FAY - Concept Martial Arts. Page 47
Brian is the founder and chief instructor of the Concept Martial Arts Academy Belfast. He has been involved in various martial arts for over forty years. He holds a black belt in Goju-Ryu karate as well as various ranks in a number of other martial arts, and is a fully certified CCU instructor in Muay Thai, Wing Chun, Jeet Kune Do, Filipino martial arts, Silat and yoga.
W: www.cmaab.uk
W: www.facebook.com/jkdbelfast

CYNTHIA MORRISON – Stage Combat. Page 153
Cynthia Morrison BA, lives in south Florida. Her academic degrees major in law and theology. She is a writer and an award-winning playwright with theatrical works featured Off-Broadway in New York City. She is also a graduate of the Burt Reynolds Institute. She is an accomplished equestrian winning international titles in the mounted combat sport of jousting and is Official Mounted Combat Adviser for the U.S. Open Polo Championships Wellington, (2005); Certified by the American Jousting Alliance (1997) as Mounted Combat Lance & Shield, Sword, Spear and Broadsword; three time international woman's jousting champion; Founding Officer, Jousting Instructor and Fight Director at the Palm Beach Jousting; a Theatrical Fight & Swordplay Instructor at the Burt Reynolds Institute, and a Bartitsu instructor.
W: www.cynthiamorrison.yolasite.com
W: www.jousting.yolasite.com

DAVID KAHN - Israeli Krav Maga. Page 83
David is the IKMA (Israeli Krav Maga Association) United States Chief Instructor and received his advanced black-belt teaching certifications from Grandmaster Haim Gidon, the world's highest ranked Krav Maga instructor. David is the only American to sit on the IKMA Board of

Directors. The United States Judo Association also awarded David a fifth degree black-belt in combat Ju-jitsu. David has trained all branches of the US military, along with the Royal Marines, including dozens of Special Operations personnel. He has also taught at many respected hand-to-hand combat schools including at the Marine Corps Martial Arts School of Excellence, Quantico, (MACE), a Navy Advance Training Command, and U.S. Army Combatives School, Fort Benning. David has also trained more than fifty federal, state, and local law enforcement agencies including having taught at the FBI Academy (Quantico), and is a certified instructor by the State of New Jersey Police Training Commission. David sponsors comprehensive civilian safety programs, and has also trained several celebrities in the Israeli method. Mainstream media regularly feature David including *Men's Fitness, GQ, USA Today, Los Angeles Times, Washington Post, New Yorker, Penthouse, Fitness, Marine Corps News, Armed Forces Network, Special Operations Report* and *Military.com*. David previously authored the books *Krav Maga, Advanced Krav Maga, Krav Maga Weapon Defenses* and *Krav Maga Professional Tactics*. He also produced the *Mastering Krav Maga* DVD series, Volumes I-IV along with the *Mastering Krav Maga Online* program. David and his partners operate several Israeli Krav Maga training centres of excellence.
W: www.israelikrav.com

JONATHAN HODGSON – Progressive Kenpo. Page 134
Jonathan Hodgson has trained in Kenpo since 1991, initially under Ben Harms. He was graded senior back belt in 2000 by Rob Walsh, and graded 1st degree black belt in 2004 by Neil Hazelland, he is currently a IV degree black belt. He has also studied numerous other systems over the years including amongst other things; fencing - foil, epee and sabre under Prof Perry, Ju-jutsu, Kobudo, Tae Kwon Do, kickboxing, Silat, Kali, Wing Chun, Taichi, Qi Gong, Taichi, historical Ninjutsu, boxing and Muay Thai. He has been teaching since 1998 and is a Level 4 Sports Coach and creator of The Kagemusha Foundation. Jonathan has also developed Applicable Blade Skills system for all styles and individual military personnel, taught weapons at Sports Coach Expo 2016, and devised the original weapons syllabus for Chard Martial Arts.
W: www.themillgym.co.uk
FB: The Kagemusha Foundation
FB: The Mill Ilminster

KEVIN O'HAGAN - Combat Ju-jutsu. Page 43
Sensei Kevin O'Hagan is fifty-five years old. He started training in martial arts as a fourteen year-old boy, training in Pak Mei White Tiger kung fu, Taekwondo, and then moved into Aikido / Aikijutsu

training directly under Japanese Sensei, before finally finding Ju-jutsu. Ju-jutsu has been his base art ever since and, although he has crossed trained in many arts, he has taught his combat Ju-jutsu in his home town of Bristol since the early '80s. Kevin at present holds a 7th Dan Master's grade in Combat Ju-jutsu, and is the highest graded instructor in the south west of England in this martial art. He also holds black belts in karate, Jutsu and Japanese Ju-jutsu, and is an ex-professional MMA fighter and full contact Ju-jutsu competitor. He is also a senior instructor with the British Combat Association, and was recently inducted into the M.I.A Hall of Fame. Kevin has travelled the world instructing, and is the author of eight books on the martial arts as well as producing several training DVDs, and in 2017 his autobiography is due for release titled: *When We Were Warriors*.
W: www.kevinohagan.com
W: www.impactgymbristol.com.

MO TEAGUE – Hard Target Combat System. Page 78
Mo has fifteen years military service as an elite infantry regiment / military intelligence analyst. He is a Master instructor in Jeet Kune Do under the late Grand Master Richard Bustillo, and has had instructorship under Rick Faye and Erik Paulson. He is also a qualified Sambo instructor under Federation of Russian Martial Arts. Mo is also a Weapons & Tactics and close protection CQB instructor.
FB: Maurice Teague

NICK MAISON – Total Krav Maga. Page 158
Nick is currently the most qualified instructor in the UK and the highest grade; Expert Level 4. He is a former director for both Krav Maga Global (KMG) and the International Krav Maga Federation (IKMF), and currently teaches instructor courses and refresher course worldwide as part of the Krav Maga Global International Team of Experts. Nick served in the British Army for fourteen years, for the last seven years Nick was a Physical Training Instructor in the army and, amongst many things, also taught unarmed combat. On leaving the army Physical Training Corps, Nick first qualified as a military Krav Maga instructor on a course hosted by the Polish Commando Brigade. He then went on to complete Krav Maga S.W.A.T., close protection, combat fighting and various other specialist instructor courses. Nick currently runs Total Krav Maga, one of the UK's longest running and most professional Krav Maga schools, under the wing of Krav Maga Global (KMG).
W: www.totalkravmaga.com

NORM WILLIS - Jeet Kune Do. Page 93
As a child Sifi Norm Willis was bullied, so his Dad taught him some

boxing. At high school in the '80s, at the age of fifteen, he joined a local boxing club which was his journey into the fighting arts. He had always been interested in boxing and martial arts and, of course, Bruce Lee was always on the TV. By the age of seventeen he had joined his first kung fu school and quickly picked up the basics. This experience gave him the thirst to learn more, develop his skills and by nineteen he had started kickboxing. Following a series of competitions, and a variety of different jobs in the security industry (the Ministry of Defence, celebrity and financial close protection, events security and night clubs), he opened his own dojo. Since then he has never looked back and training others is now his vocation, and his base is teaching the skills and experience he has picked up over the years from real-life situations. As a martial arts instructor, he has trained people from all walks of life including - but not limited to - members of the Ministry of Defence, police and fire service, military and security personnel. He teaches kickboxing, grappling, Krav Maga, Eskrima, Wing Chun and Jeet Kune Do. He is a 4th dan black belt, a qualified kickboxing instructor, Krav Maga instructor, Self-defence instructor, a black belt Dacayana Eskrima instructor, a Wing Chun kung fu instructor, a 3rd generation Jeet Kune Do instructor, and a Level 3 Personal Trainer.
W: www.centrelineacademy.com

PAUL 'ROCK' HIGGINS – V.I.P.A. Tactical Training System.
Page 165

Paul 'Rock' Higgins CMAS SAC Dipi is a Certified Master Anti-Terrorism Specialist who has worked in the close protection industry for the last twenty-five years, with nine years military service prior to moving into the protection industry. Paul provides company directors, managers and staff members with anti-terrorism training while developing operating procedures helping to mitigate risks and threats from many forms of attack and man-made and natural disasters. Paul started training in combat arts in 1978 and to continues to train with world class instructors from many diverse combative formats. Paul has taught thousands of civilians, bodyguards, military and law enforcement personnel in combat disciplines for their personal lives or for their duties in their professional employment. While in the military, Paul instructed close quarter combat to troops going up against Russian Spetsnaz special forces and airborne forces, and various terrorist organisations alongside instructing military personnel in weapon handling, combat tactics and CBRNE (Chemical Biological Radiological Nuclear Explosive) warfare. Paul is a graduate of the Professional Bodyguard Association, an ex-military Close Quarter Combat Instructor, he holds black belts and instructor qualifications in various combat systems, is a registered self-protection instructor

with the British Combat Association, a self-defence instructor with the Self-Defence Federation and an ABA assistant boxing coach.
W: www.vipatacticaltraining.com

PETER ELLIS - Sphere Combat Systems. Page 150
Peter holds a 7th degree black sash – Sphere Combat (Grandmaster Grade), 7th degree black sash - kung fu (Master Grade), 2nd dan black belt - Krav Maga (Instructor) and high-ranking grades in several other systems including, Aikido, Silat, Kali, Jeet Kun Do, Thai Boxing and full contact karate. Peter has been training in martial arts / close quarter combat since he was just twelve years-old, and began instructing in his early twenties. Due to his passion and never ending pursuit of excellence Peter as a career spanning over four decades. Training throughout his career with world renowned instructors. Peter's Sphere Combat Systems was an evolution from his traditional martial arts training and unconventional combat training, in which Peter is highly graded, and the need to develop a close quarter combat system that could be used by all, from Special Forces operatives to individuals wanting to learn how to protect themselves and their loved ones.
W: www.sphere-tactical-training.com
W: www.sphereprotectionservices.com
FB: www.facebook.com/groups/196360553786936/

RUSSELL JARMESTY - MeanStreets Self-Defence. Page 115
Russell is the founder of MeanStreets Self-Defence, co-founder of the online *Martial Arts Guardian* magazine, and the Director of MSDA (MeanStreets Self Defence Association). He is also owner and Chief Instructor at Jarmesty Martial Arts Academy where he teaches over two hundred students, five nights a week. Russ is 3rd dan and received his black-belts from Hanshi Trevor Roberts. In 2016, his *Brutal Bouncer* DVD box-set won Self-Defence DVD of the Year at the British Martial Arts awards, where he also received self-defence Instructor of the Year.
W: www.jarmestymartialarts.com

SIMON MORRELL - Fight Fortress. Page 71
Simon has trained in combat arts for thirty-six years, and currently holds the rank of 6th dan black belt in Concepts of Krav Maga, kickboxing and practical karate (BCA & WMO registered). He is also a qualified wrestling coach under the BAWA, and a member of the Kizuna Brotherhood, conceived in 1968 by Ronnie Colwell, one of the founding fathers of British karate and British Ju-jutsu, and now with members worldwide. Simon is also the author of six books, including his autobiography: *Bullied to Black Belt*, currently in development as

a British feature film.
W: www.simonmorrell.com
FB: www.facebook.com/SimonMorrellMartialArt
T: @simonmorrell
W: www.kizunabrotherhood.com

STEVEN TIMPERLEY - Knives & Edged Weapons Awareness Programme (KEWAP). Page 102

Steven is a former UK military specialist instructor, Founder of KEWAP (Knives & Edged Weapons Awareness Programme), and PST (Personal Safety Training). Steven is also the President of the UK Martial Arts Alliance, a unique network of martial arts instructors and personal safety trainers.
W: www.eliteresponsetraining.co.uk
W: www.kewap.org.uk
W: www.ukmaa.org
W: www.facebook.com/steven.timperley1

STEVE TAPPIN - Escrima Concepts. Page 64

As a child, Steve's martial art training mainly consisted of boxing and wrestling; he first trained with his family and friends, and then went on to a few gyms, but it took many years for him to find out where he belonged. In the early '70s Steve wanted to gain knowledge about kicking so started training karate under Sensei Charles Mack in Holborn, which was his first introduction into Eastern Martial Arts. Looking back, Steve wished he had stayed longer with him, but life was calling and he was young and naïve, and about to enter the ugly world of the streets. In 1976, his friend John Sullivan (AKA Scully) invited him to train in Escrima and was taken to Brian Jones club where they free-sparred and trained with weapons. In 1978 he attended Bill Newman's (Brian Jones' student) club, a very aggressive no nonsense sparring and weapons training club. Steve's initial passion was free-sparring and over the years he visited many clubs away from home to test himself and to see how he did against other arts and in other environments. He also ran his own clubs teaching weapons and unarmed free-sparing, with all styles welcomed to attend to test their arts. In the late '70s and early '80s, and then later on in the '90s Steve would still occasionally trained privately with Scully and another friend Danny Abbott, testing, analysing and developing their art; there were only a few Escrima clubs at around that time and, as they came from the first Escrima Club in Europe, they had very little to compare their art to, apart from their own experiences and testing themselves for weaknesses and strengths and the ability to work within hostile and aggressive environments. Alongside Steve's martial arts, from 1979 Steve also trained with

ancient and medieval weapons, which lead him to Roy King and from Roy onto others including John Waller who, in Steve's opinion, was one of the best sword and weapon's masters at that time; his knowledge, skill, intent and serious attitude (with humour) set him above many others. After decades of training and teaching around the world, in 2001 Steve founded Escrima Concepts and went independent in 2003, teaching mainly in western Europe.
W: www.escrimaconcepts.com
FB: Eecrima Concepts

TONY SOMERS - Real Combat System. Page 144
Tony Somers is Joint Chief Instructor of the Real Combat System. He is 6th dan Real Combat System, 1st dan Combat Ju-jitsu, 1st dan Shotokan karate, as well as a qualified life coach and counsellor.
W: www.realcombatsystem.co.uk
W: www.anthonysomers.com

TYRREL FRANCIS – Karate and Muay Thai. Pages 97 & 125
Tyrrel is an author, personal trainer and boxing coach, holds a 2nd dan black belt in Shotokan karate, as well as a 3rd degree black belt in kickboxing. An experienced competitor in Muay Thai, K1 kickboxing and boxing events, he is a former member of the WPKA England kickboxing team, as well as a former Royal Navy karate champion, British WPKA kickboxing and WAKO kickboxing champion, and currently holds a WCBC boxing English title.
FB: Tyrrel Francis

YURI KOSTROV - Agni Kempo. Page 22
Agni Kempo Grandmaster and martial artist Yuri Kostrov began training at the age of ten in Kiev, Ukraine. At the age of twelve he studied SAMBO under the founder of the SAMBO in the Ukraine, Roman Aleksandrovich Shkolnikov. In 1965 he started studying judo and in 1971, during his military service, Yuri studied Shotokan, Goju-Ryu and Kyokushinkai karate, as well as Wing Chun Yip Man. From 1976 to 1986, he studied Shang Dao Quan Gongfu under the guidance of master Guo Yu. In 1984 he developed his own style Agni Kempo Universal Fist Fight, a highly developed system of counteraction between an unarmed and armed individuals
W: www.kostrov.org.ua
W: www.facebook.com/kostrov
W: www.plus.google.com/u/0/+GrandmasterSokeYuriyKostrov

VIRGIL O. CAVADA - Eskrima. Page 29
Master Virgil Cavada was born in Catmon, Cebu, Philippines in 1954. Has a degree in Mechanical Engineering. He is also a Certified Sports

Nutrition Specialist and a Personal Trainer. Virgil started learning in Eskrima while in college in 1973, when a fellow weightlifter introduced it to him. His system of Applied Eskrima specialises in close quarters, using blunt weapons, bladed weapons and then empty hands applications. He also teaches how to combine both the long-range and short-range methods of Eskrima. The main focus of Applied Eskrima training is for reflex speed development and retention. Master Virgil Cavada has a training centre in West Covina, California, USA and Catmon, Cebu, Philippines. He travels around the world to conduct private trainings and group seminars.
W: www.appliedeskrima.com
W: www.eskrimachannel.com
FB: Virgil O. Cavada
Instagram: BunalSugbo

Introduction

About this Book

With this book, I have decided to just focus on twenty-four urban self-defence and close quarter combat systems mainly for two reasons; firstly, during my initial research, I found over two hundred different combat styles, and that wasn't including the many traditional martial arts practised around the world today and all their variations. So, instead of a very brief, bite-size chapter on each, which doesn't give you very much information at all, I wanted to explore far fewer styles but in much more detail, which I think is really important, especially for anyone looking for something more specific; it is better to know a lot more about a few systems, than to know very little about a lot.

Secondly, this book isn't written by me, but by professional instructors and Sensei around the world and, to be honest, it would have been virtually impossible to get over two hundred professionals to write a detailed chapter on their specialised system – it was hard enough getting twenty-four and for some systems and styles it was almost impossible to find someone willing to write about them and, like all books, I had to have a deadline and I had to have a limit to the number of people I asked for each style. Some people were extremely proud of their system and wanted to tell as many other people as possible about it, whereas others either repeatedly ignored my requests (as so many people now seem to do with emails) or quickly declined; for whatever reason they seemed not to want to tell *anyone* about their system.

But actually, I think twenty-four is a really good number and just enough to not get lost or confused as to what sort of systems and styles there are out there, and what they can (or can't) do. Saying that though, I might (and it is just a '*might*') compile a Volume 2 with more interesting combat styles should I have enough interest, both from other renown professionals willing to profile themselves and showcase their systems, and from people wanting to read about them.

Lastly... I have showcased Krav Maga twice, from two different professionals; *Israeli Krav Maga* by David Khan in the USA, and *Total Krav Maga* from Nick Maison in the UK, both at the very top of their game and considered the highest grades in this style in each of these countries. Krav Maga has influenced almost every other form of Urban Combat in the world today, so it is worth spotlighting these two professionals and their system in more detail. I have also profiled KENPO and its more progressive system KENPO, as well as Escrima and its more modern variation Eskrima, again because both of these styles have developed and significantly influenced the martial arts and self-defence world today.

What Makes a Really Good Combat Specialist?

The people featured in this book are undoubtedly some of the very best in the business; quite simply, they have dedicated their lives to self-defence and combat training. I absolutely believe that most people can do most things in life really, really well; they just need to *want it* enough, and the reason why most people don't achieve is just because they don't want to achieve. Most of the limits we have set in our lives, and on ourselves, are self-imposed limits; we find excuses and reasons for *not* doing things rather than finding ways *of* doing things. But, as we often witness, ordinary people really have gone on to do extraordinary things and, after reading about each of the individual contributors in this book and the development of their specific styles - or their practice of a more traditional style - two words immediately spring to mind when trying to understand what makes people become really, really good combat specialists; COMMITMENT and PASSION. Dojos, training academies, sports halls and gyms are full of martial artists and combat specialists training hard, rehearsing and practising, week in, week out, which is undeniably brilliant, but it is commitment and real passion that makes just a very few stand out, and from those that stand out, only a very small handful eventually become some of the very best. It isn't that others don't have commitment and passion, of course they do, but there is another level that drives some people to become the best of the best within the combat world.

Finding the Right Combat System

We are all different and we all want different things in life. However, until we actually try different things in life, we often don't know what we want in life! And the same goes for combat training; there are so many martial arts, self-defence and urban combat systems out there, the hardest thing is finding the right system for our needs, and a system we feel most comfortable with. So how do we go about it?

Firstly, you must ask yourself *why* do you need to learn a combat system? Do you live in a tough urban environment with a high crime rate and so you need to learn a combat system purely to defend yourself against a possible threat or attack? Do you work the doors and need a combat system to help protect yourself in an often violent world, and to keep yourself, and others safe? Are you in the forces or military and therefore need more weapons based training? Or is it just for your own personal and physical growth and development?

Secondly, once you have decided *why* you want to train, you need to be honest and ask yourself *what* sort of training and environment you feel most comfortable with? Are you a wrestler or grappler and feel comfortable up close and personal? Or do you prefer the rigidity and relative isolation of the kata? Are you a fairly aggressive person and feel more at ease with tough sparring and full-contact, or do you prefer more sport based, less contact styles? By trying different styles and systems you will quickly understand what you want out of your combat training, and once you know what you want, you can then start to set yourself goals, and start to work towards achieving those goals - there are styles and systems featured in this book that suit just about everyone.

And **thirdly**, you should *always* choose an instructor that is dedicated in helping you learn, grow and develop; learning any form of combat isn't easy; it's tough and it's hard work, and it takes time and a lot of commitment, especially in the first few months as you are settling into a new environment, so find an instructor that pushes you to learn, but is patient too. Find and instructor that believes in you.

Be The Best You Can Be

If someone ask you what you do for a living, you wouldn't tell them that you were an *average* carpenter, or an *average* lawyer, or an *average* accountant, or an *average* soldier, or an *average* doorman (or woman). No one wants to be *average,* and no one wants to tell others that they are *average* either! So treat your combat training in the same way... *don't be average*! Develop a real COMMITMENT and PASSION towards your chosen system or style, study hard, ask lots of questions, learn from others, be respectful, take advice, read combat books and watch combat movies, buy combat DVDs and watch YouTube techniques of your chosen style; dedicate yourself to learning and dedicate yourself to being the very best you can be.

In fact be *better* than you ever thought you could be!

Train Hard, Stay Tough
Robin

A Professionals' Guide to 24 Urban Self-Defence and Close Quarter Combat Systems

AGNI KEMPO – Surviving Real-Life Combat
By Yuri Kostrov
Translated from Russian into English by Inna Zabrodskaya

Grandmaster of Sport and martial artist Yuri Kostrov began training at the age of ten in Kiev, Ukraine. He was selected to enter the boxing section of the Olympic reserve school which belonged to the Dynamo sports club. At the age of twelve he picked up SAMBO (an acronym for SAMozashchita Bez Oruzhiya) in the Locomotive sports club, and was trained under the supervision of the founder of the SAMBO in the Ukraine, Roman Aleksandrovich Shkolnikov. In 1965, Yuri also joined with the newly organised judo group. In 1971, during his military service, Yuri got familiar with karate and began his career as an expert of martial arts. He independently studied such styles of karate including Shotokan, Goju-Ryu and Kyokushinkai, as well as the Hong Kong style Wing Chun Yip Man. From 1976 to 1986, he studied the family style of Shang Dao Quan Gongfu under the guidance of master Guo Yu An. However, the knowledge he acquired during his studies did not satisfy Yuri's character. As he discovered; in judo there was practically no technique of striking the opponent, and in karate, no technique of throwing. Plus little attention was paid to fighting an armed enemy. So in 1984 he began developing his own system. It developed into a universal system which includes focusing on highly developing the counteraction between an unarmed and armed individuals. During the same period, Yuri got acquainted with the *Teachings of Agni Yoga*. After thinking it over, Yuri came up with the philosophical foundation for his style which he named Agni Kempo Universal Fist Fight.

In 1987, Yuri completed working on the foundations of his style but the system's improvement continued and is being perfected all the time.

Agni Kempo is not considered a system of sports fights. Most of the techniques are aimed at survival and causing radical physical damage to the enemy in real-life combat. Followers of Agni Kempo have competed in various styles of martial arts and have became European and International champions in Kyokushinkai karate, Asihara karate, Ju-jitsu, etc.

Currently the main direction is training civilians, the Ukrainian army, police forces and Special Forces to survive in counteractions with a real aggressor. To this end, the martial arts of Agni Kempo are divided into four systems:

1. Professional - for civilians.

2. Bridge - for young people with weakened health and elderly people.

3. PUMA - for special police units, customs and border guards.

4. BARS - for Special Forces, police and security services.

Grandmaster Yuri Kostrov continues perfecting his martial arts style Agni Kempo. He trains himself and develops new and modern techniques for the training process to educate and train new masters of Agni Kempo - the black belts. He also continues working on the multi-volume textbook on Agni Kempo. In the future, Yuri will focus on passing his knowledge and experience to his grandchildren, as well as promoting the style in other countries.

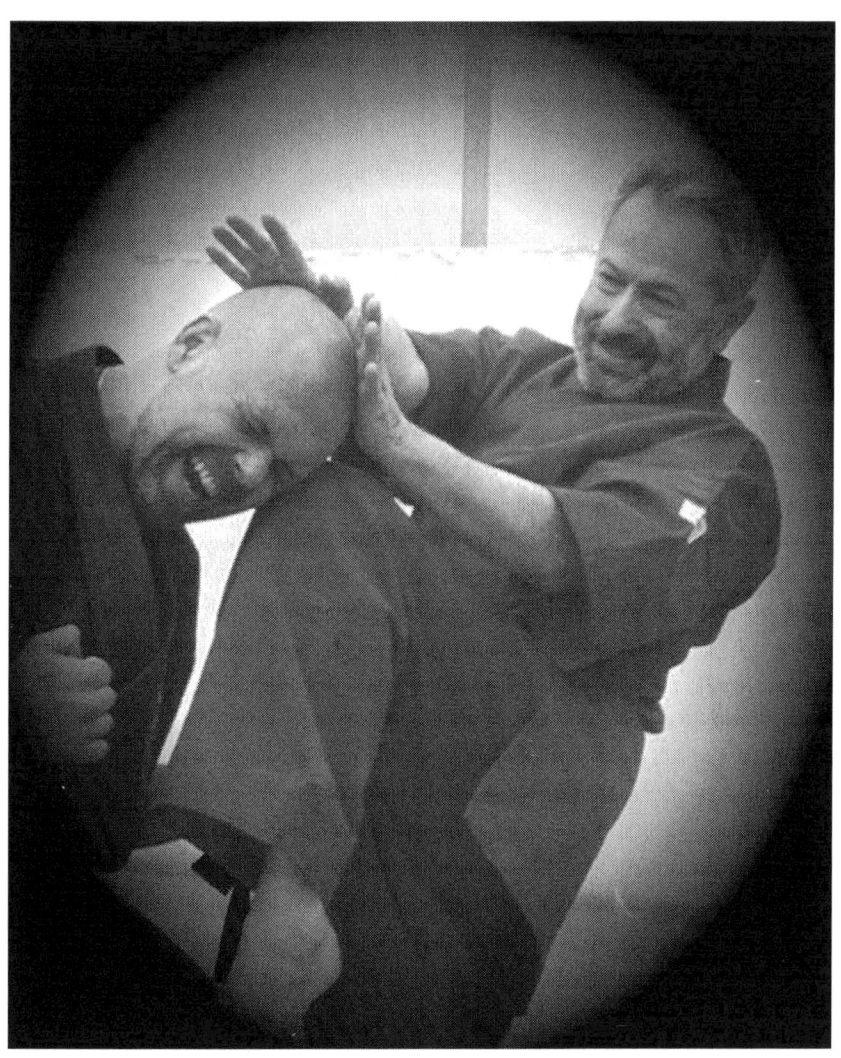

APPLIED ESKRIMA – Developing the Reflex Speed of the Student
By Virgil Cavada

Eskrima or Arnis - these names are practically the same and are used depending what part of the Philippines this art is being trained in. From when I was a young boy up until now, Eskrima or Arnis are the two most popular names used, even if there are often other more local names depending on location.

Eskrima or Arnis is just under a big umbrella called Filipino martial arts. Filipino martial arts has; stand-up grappling, ground fighting, boxing (panantukan or suntokan), bladed weapons fighting and other empty hands systems with influences from neighbouring countries. Most Eskrima or Arnis systems also have their own blunt weapons, bladed weapons and bare hands applications.

Eskrima or Arnis is mainly divided in two ranges or distances. The first one is the Long Range, in which the main focus is to disable the hand-holding the weapon and, once that is done, will come in to finish off the opponent. The main focus of the long range system of Eskrima is footwork, timing and distancing.

The second is the Short or Close Range in which the opponent is within an arms-length distance during the fight. In short range, a lot of body weapons are used in Eskrima when using the empty hands applications; hands, elbows, knees, feet and head are commonly employed during the empty hands fight. During the bladed weapons portion, all types of bladed weapons are taught and used, but the most commonly used bladed weapon is the knife with lengths from four to eight inches.

In the blunt weapons area, rattan sticks are the mostly used for training. The rattan stick lengths vary from 24 to 36 inches.

Some say, there is also a Medium Range, but I call the Medium Range a transition distance between the long and short ranges.

During World War II, since the Philippines was still under American control, a Battalion of Filipino soldiers were formed and one of the weapon issued to each one of the soldiers was a Bolo. The blade length alone is from twelve to sixteen inches. The Bolo is a multi-purpose tool and until today, it is still the main tool for Filipinos mostly in the countryside. The Bolo can cut, slice, stab, use to dig and more.

I began my Eskrima training in 1973 when I was nineteen years-old. I trained in a system called Balintawak; a short or close range system of Eskrima. It uses a single stick in one hand, while the other hand is used for several functions; holding, pushing, punching, blocking, disarming, grabbing, poking.

In 2010, I formed Applied Eskrima for the main purpose of spreading the martial arts that I had trained in for such a long time. The main focus of the system is to develop the reflex speed of the student. It is accomplish by specific drills and other lessons. Realistic and functional sparring is also part of the training, with emphasis on footwork, distancing and speed.

I also teach how to effectively combined the positives of both the long range system and the close range system, because whoever has the ability to come in and out of ranges during a fight has a very big advantage. Whether it be in the ring or on the streets, a person who has the ability to utilize distance to his advantage, will always have a big edge.

Applied Eskrima has a total of 10 Modules. Each Module has at least twenty-six lessons and each lesson is connected to the next. The lessons are practical and functional, and builds the students' ability physically and mentally.

Module 1 is primarily the Basics Module. This is where stances, forms, striking patterns, history, footwork, speed drills, basic disarms, reflex speed drills, basic empty hands blocks, holding counters, and more are introduced. The amount of time required to master Module 1 varies from student to student.

I also encourage my students to take notes because taking notes heightens the learning process and will eventually be very convenient in the future, if that student decides to teach.

Applied Eskrima ranks its students according to their knowledge and after each Module completion the student has a choice to take a test or not. If a student decides not to take they can continue learning the next Module and so on. If the student decides to take the test, they will be given it in three phases: written, verbal and practical. Only a total of nine mistakes are allowed in the three phases. The maximum time allotted for the written test is three hours.

Because I totally believe on self-preservation, Applied Eskrima is a defensive system first and foremost. However, with a knowledge of Applied Eskrima, attacking or doing offensive moves are also very easy. In the initial stages of learning Applied Eskrima, sticks are the primary tools where the student is taught the proper stances and control. Proper stances and control are two very important traits because the ultimate goal is fast sparring with footwork. The student must be able to stop his or her strike halfway, so that the person in front, or their sparring partner, will not get hit. In regular training, we only wear eye protectors, and sometimes hand gloves, which is why knowing how to control a hit or a strike is very important. Once a month we also do freestyle sparring where both sides wear helmets and body protector vests so that both sides can then strike their opponent to their hearts-content.

Once the student has the basics of footwork and control, his journey becomes a lot easier and more advance lessons are introduced and speed and power increased.

Advance techniques like disarming and knowing how to counter disarms are standard advanced lessons. Focusing on controlling the opponent is also taught and, of course, knowing how to counter if the opponent tries to impose control moves on you. Control moves can be in the form of trapping and disabling one part of your body, or simply by taking away your balance.

After mastering the use of the single stick, the student will then learn different variations of sparring, so instead of using one stick, they now uses two sticks, or use one stick and their sparring partner uses two sticks. Using a training knife or bolo will then follow and then knowing the empty hands applications for all those lessons. And all the while, the right hand is the main hand used for training and, once the student is competent on using the right hand, training will then start with left hand as the main hand holding the weapon. There are so many advantages if the student knows how to use weapons properly, with both the left and right hands. For example: when holding a weapon with just one hand, eventually that hand tires and so, with the other hand trained, it is a big plus. Also, when the primary hand gets injured in training – or in real life - having a trained other hand makes it much easier to fight and therefore to survive. Using interchangeable left and right hands can also distract or confuse an opponent. Since the majority of the people in the world are right-handed, Applied Eskrima focuses on improving or enhancing the left-hand reflex speed but of course, left-handed people can focus on improving their right-hand reflex speed. Once the weapons training is done, knowing Empty Hands or Bare Hands Applications becomes so much easier.

One of the big advantages of Applied Eskrima is fast sparring within arms length, using more than one-hundred different types of sparring variables. One of the main focuses during sparring is cognitive training, and I have developed a way on how to add cognitive training while doing drills or sparring.

The curriculum and all of the great techniques of Applied Eskrima are useless without one main ingredient: The Student. The student, will not improve, nor learn, nor master Applied Eskrima, and will not be able to use Applied Eskrima to its full potential without one factor: Regular Training. Without regular training, students cannot be good. However becoming Experts or Masters is not just about the number of hours training or years of training, but students must train efficiently and with quality material. Efficient training must be done on a regular and consistent basis, and mainly focusing on weak areas, or areas that need improvement. Students must also take care of their bodies so that it can handle the stress put on it during serious training.

Lastly, students must also train their minds on how and when to use their martial arts ability.

> *"If you can do sparring using a thirty-inch long stick within arms length from your sparring partner, Can you imagine how fast and good you will be, with just your bare hands, doing the same thing, with the same distance...?"*

Eskrima is currently being trained worldwide in over thirty-five countries.

AWARENESS RESPONSE DELIVERY (ARD) - As Street Related as Realistically Possible

By Adam Parsons

Over twenty-five years of studying the martial arts, my love of learning took me through many of the traditional styles and systems, including becoming a practitioner of Bartitsu and setting up the UK Bartitsu Alliance (see section on Bartitsu page 39). I studied what suited me best and how I felt the flow of movements kept as an extension of my own natural movement. Not just to be that unstoppable warrior I had dreamed of being as a child, but also to embrace my ever growing love of learning in the area, and the serenity and balance that came with training.

I developed my own training regime, including twenty minute runs at a ten-minute mile pace three times a week, and a one hour run at the same pace at the weekend, including strike training against solid trees in the park twice a week, to make sure of my form and commitment to the hit, often bruising myself badly until I found the correct way to deliver each strike. In the gym or dojo, training also included wrestling with larger guys once a week to keep a check on my ability to unbalance a bigger, heavier attacker. I tried my best to keep myself focused and in fact I still use much of those early training methods in my training today.

I had been training in so many styles, for so long, and had some practical experience with periods defending myself during times of homelessness on the street and in the pub trade and so, after sounding out some interest, I started to develop the ARD (Awareness Response Delivery) System. ARD incorporated the flows and simple fast defence and footwork of styles such as Aikido and judo, with the more devastating strikes of Muay Thai and karate, as well as some good old fashioned 'gutter fighting.' Due to a worry about realism, rather than just an ego trip, ARD developed over time into its own unique and specific style with written and tested syllabus, membership of an international body, insurance to teach this new system, and the development of the ARD instructor training program.

I separated the style into three distinct levels, each building on the last:

Level 1 – An attack by a drunk person using their strength to counter through.

Level 2 – Building on level 1 but this time with focus on a sober attacker.

Level 3 – Building on levels 1 and 2, but focusing on an attacker who can fight and who is likely have some 'dirty' street fighting techniques and experience.

Each level looks at the style of attack possible, and the appropriate defensive movements, all however with the same baseline in solid object strikes, flowing locks, footwork and continual forward movement. Another condition of my training is that it must be done in normal street clothing, not gym or dojo clothing, reflecting a real street attack and the ability to react appropriately and instantly, which otherwise could be devastating and even potentially life-threatening.

Street style combat training should be street style and, with a growing body of students from all walks of life and professions, I am developing ARD to be a street related as realistically possible.

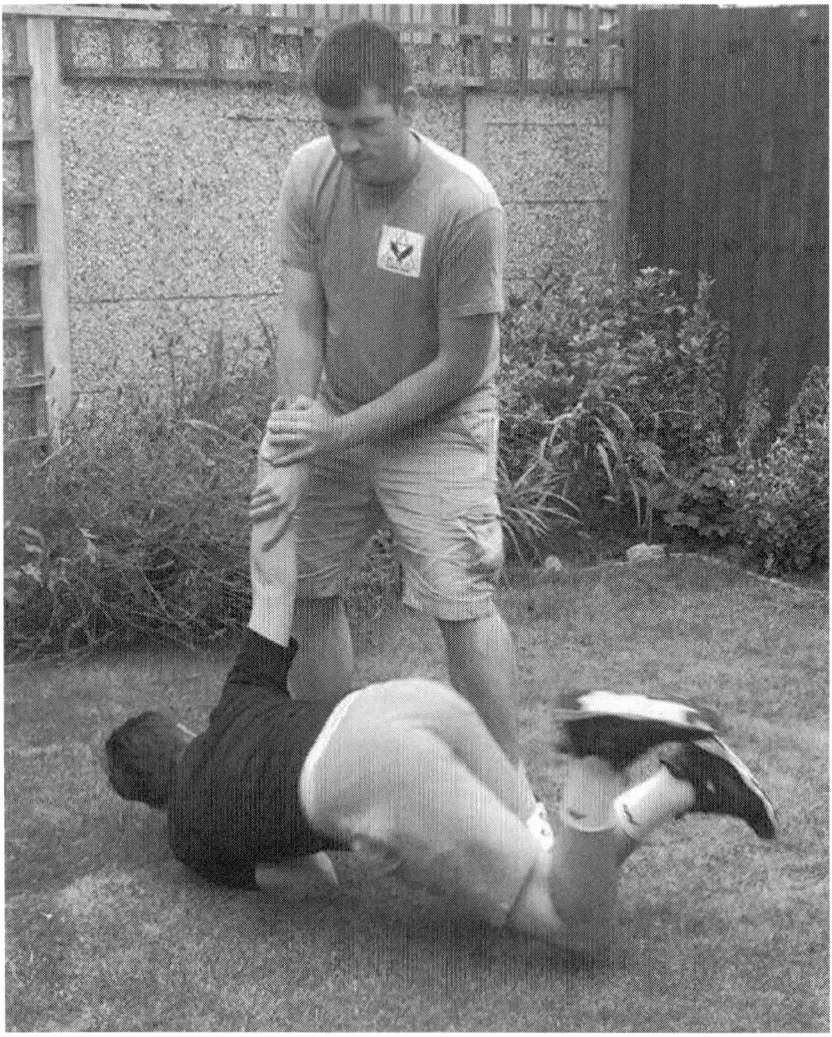

BARTITSU - A Fighting Style for Gentleman

By Adam Parsons of the UKBA

After studying in martial arts since I was four, with a baseline in judo then moving onto Aikido as well as other styles, and taking part in several tournaments, I became a boxing and self-defence instructor through the Self Defence Federation, as well as the All Styles Martial Arts Association. I then started training in, and then instructing, Bartitsu.

Bartitsu? What the hell is that? That's the usual response to what I do along with a giggle at the name and an assumption that I've made it up.

Just for the record, I didn't.

Bartitsu is a wonderful and variable martial art that is becoming more and more recognized far beyond scenes in *The Sherlock Holmes* and *Kingsman* films.

Bartitsu, in my humble opinion, has one of the most interesting histories of all the martial arts systems, although that term itself does not sit perfectly due to a far less codified and changing approach the system expresses.

Although generally labelled as a British martial art and a fighting style for gentleman, its origins and usage do not entirely fall in line with this assumptive summation. The system was created by E.W. Barton-Wright, a martial arts enthusiast and journalist (also world traveller with various other employments). As an enthusiast of the martial arts and human physicality, in Tokyo, and elsewhere, Barton-Wright studied variations of Ju-jutsu and more. Upon returning to England in early 1898, Barton-Wright believed there was a more effective approach that could be taken for the harsh streets of Victorian London and so, combined the styles he had learned, formed his own method of self-defence training, which he called Bartitsu.

Over the next two years, he also added elements of British boxing, French Savate and the La Canne stick fighting style of Swiss master Pierre Vigny.

In 1900, Barton-Wright established the Bartitsu School of Arms and

Physical Culture at 67b Shaftesbury Avenue in London's Soho district. The school offered classes in a range of self-defence disciplines and combat sports, as well as various physical therapies involving the electrical application of heat, light, vibration and radiation. Club members included soldiers, athletes, actors, politicians and even some aristocrats. As there was much scepticism at the time to this 'foreign way of fighting,' in the following years Barton-Wright organised numerous exhibitions of self-defence techniques and promoted tournament competitions throughout London, in which his Bartitsu Club champions were challenged by wrestlers, boxers and the like to show the effectiveness of this, 'new way of fighting.'

In 1901, Barton-Wright published additional articles that detailed the Bartitsu method of fighting with a walking stick or umbrella. The belief that this style was one for gentleman came from the fact that after much outcry from fans, in *The Adventure of the Empty House*, Sir Arthur Conan Doyle, the author of the Sherlock Holmes stories, who had worked on the *Pearson* magazine with Barton-Wright, referred to Bartitsu (misspelled as "Baritsu") in explaining how Holmes had defeated Professor Moriarty after the final conflict at the Reichenbach Falls.

So why has there been so little recognition of this exciting style that suggests itself to perhaps be the conceptual grandparent to MMA and the UFC?

Well this is something that has a variety of explanations, but the one which seems to hold the most water is that Barton-Wright simply wasn't a very good promoter. Having overestimated the wealth of Londoners at the time, and lacking in specific business acumen, this lead to the closure of the Bartitsu Club and subsequently the disappearance of Bartitsu itself until the late 20th Century and the developing awareness of Historical European Marital Arts (HEMA), although it was rumoured that Barton-Wright gave private lessons and developed Bartitsu further into the 1920s, long after the club and more recognizable style had all but died. However, since then, the Bartitsu community has grown exponentially, not just in the UK but worldwide, with marital artists to boxers, combat specialists and street fighters from every kind of background joining its ranks.

Much of the credit for this must go to instructors such as Tony Wolf in America, who set up the Bartitsu Society; a blog like society that gives help to martial arts clubs and historical researchers, as well as writing two compendiums on Bartitsu and travelling extensively giving seminars and lectures on the subject. Also of note in bringing

Bartitsu into recognition is British instructor James Marwood who has written many great articles on the style, and uploaded videos of Bartitsu to YouTube, as well as the formation United Kingdom Bartitsu Alliance in 2015, with the express mission to help form a national association to look after the study and continued exposure of this once lost style.

The society has gone from strength to strength and now exists in several countries in three continents, with its members helping to develop the art further.

The way in which individuals study and practice this system varies widely, generally due to the background of the individual and own specific usage of the style, however, the viewpoint of the UKBA is that as long as the concepts and approaches of Bartitsu are expressly observable, any development will be acknowledged according to the individual's own martial arts or combat background.

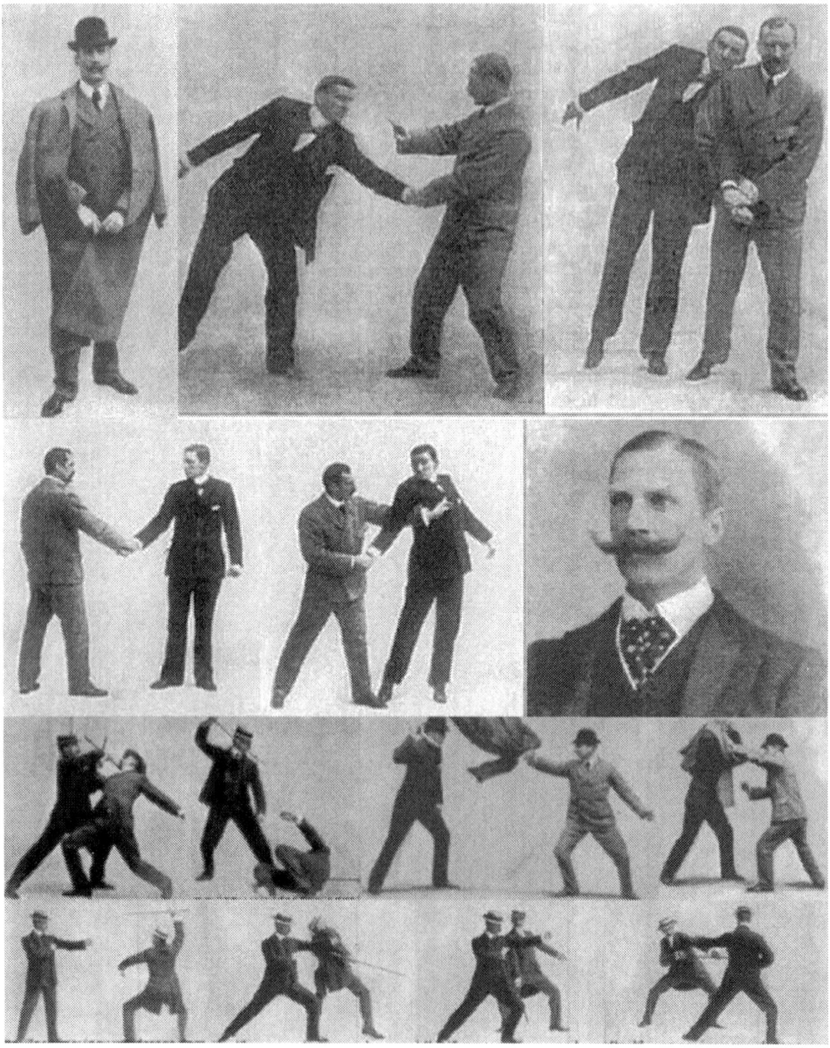

COMBAT JU-JUTSU... From the Battlefields to the Streets

By Kevin O'Hagan

If you mention the word Ju-jutsu to people, currently most of them will reply: "Oh, yeah that's that ground grappling stuff you see in the UFC." Now there is some truth to this statement, and the martial art of Brazilian Ju-jutsu has certainly proven itself in that arena countless times over. But to 'pigeon hole' all Ju-jutsu styles as 'that ground grappling stuff' is doing the art a grave injustice.

Japanese Ju-jutsu is a complete combat system of armed and unarmed techniques. It origins can be traced some 2500 years. It originally was the battlefield art of the fearsome Samurai warriors. Ground fighting was only a small part of this art, as going to the floor in real combat would have proved fatal. Japanese Ju-jutsu, in its true form, was more concerned about taking their enemy to the ground and dispatching them with a blade or bare-handed strikes. Trips and sweeps were prevalent, along with kicks to the knees, head butts and elbow strikes. Joint breaking to disarm weapons was used along with chokes and strangles to dispatch the enemy. As mentioned previously rolling around on the ground was the last resort.

My Combat Ju-jutsu system is a hybrid of the 'old school' Samurai Ju-jutsu. It holds the core principle of 80% of technique is standing and 20% on the ground. Which is really the total opposite of the BJJ philosophy. I believe many of the so-called modern combat system have their roots somewhere in Ju-jutsu, whether they realise it or not. There is nothing new in the world of martial arts, it's just be repackaged and resold to the general public looking for the next best thing.

My Combat Ju-jutsu is for purely self-protection. My former Sensei's were from military and body-guarding backgrounds, so they adapted their Ju-jutsu for the urban combat arena. Many of my peers are unfortunately no longer with us, or have retired, and I have gradually moved up the pecking order - so to speak - so that I am one of only a handful of instructors in the UK teaching true Combat Ju-jutsu.

Combat Ju-jutsu deals with today's modes of attack and deals heavily against street weapons and multiple attacks. Also, it promotes and uses pre-emptive attacking techniques as well as defensive tactics. It also works within a scale of the level of force you use, to the level of danger you are faced. Sometimes a simple wrist lock will suffice, where on other occasions it has to be a knockout or a choke to end the encounter. The system is flowing and not rigid or fixed, and it works on the concept that real combat is ever changing, and you must adapt with it. You can't work on the principle of one attack is answered with one defence. Also, it works its techniques primarily up close and in your face, where most violence starts. Any further away and you have a choice to run.

Combat Ju-jutsu includes strikes, kicks, knees, elbows and head-butts as well as throws, take-downs, joint locks and breaks, strangles, chokes, pressure points, modern adapted weaponry and a whole host of 'dirty' fighting techniques.

It also works on the principle of learn to fight on the floor but don't go to the floor to fight. Once you are on the floor you are looking to finish the situation quickly and get back to your feet. There are too many unpredictable possibilities when on the floor in real combat and not sport. Most BJJ currently now leans heavily towards sport, where pinning and position takes precedence over submission and finishing.

I love all Ju-jutsu styles but I try to keep adapting and moving with the times. I still like to keep a lineage back to how the techniques were originally trained by the Samurai and how they have adapted over the decades to blend in with ever changing times.

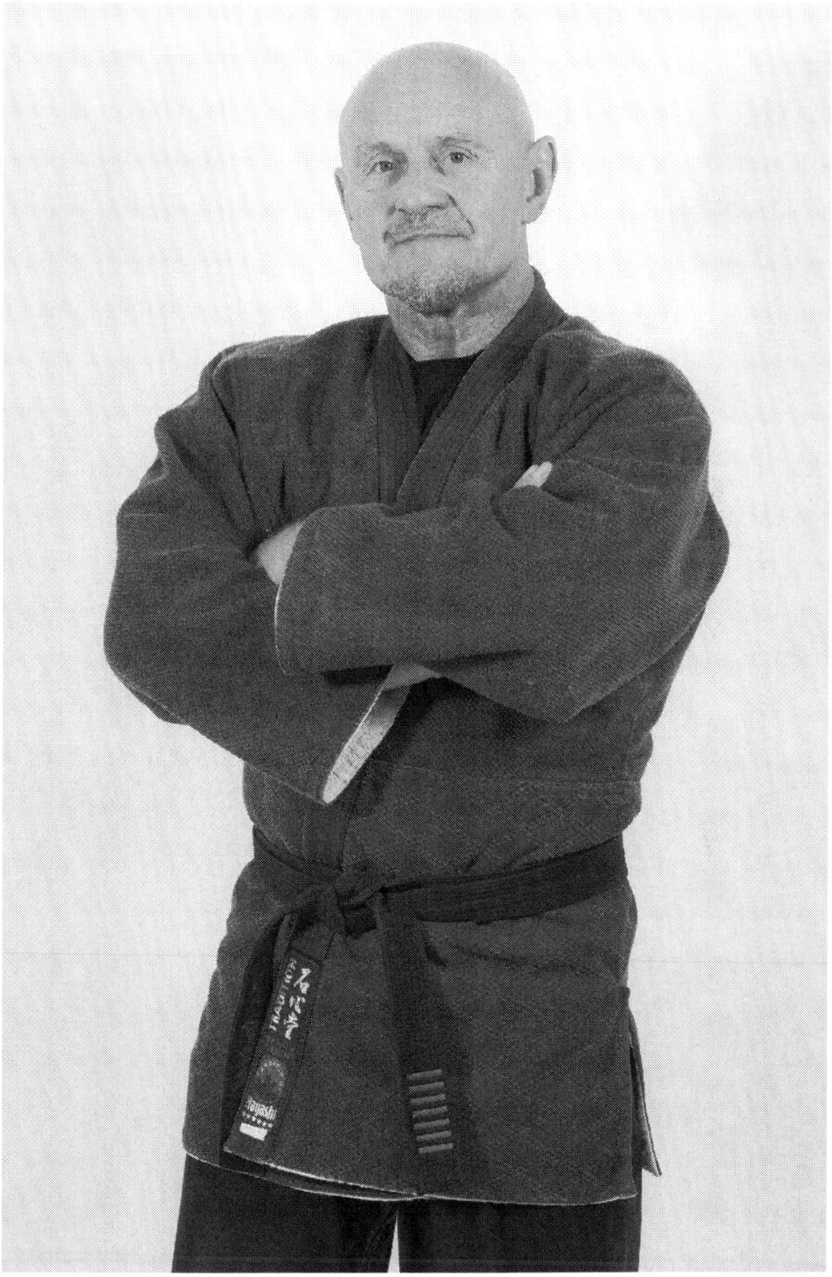

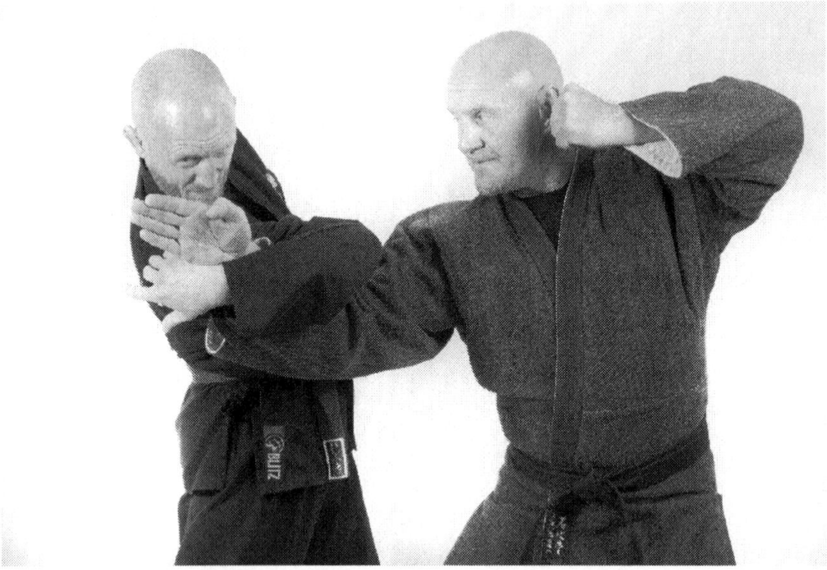

CONCEPT MARTIAL ARTS - An Idea, or a Way with No Way

By Brian Fay

My martial arts journey started way back in 1973, the year Bruce Lee died. I had never heard of him before his death, but soon found out a lot more after the flood of newspapers articles, magazines and TV programmes that followed his death and, by using and adapting his philosophies, Bruce Lee still continues to play a important role in my life to this day.

My first martial art was judo. My father took me along with my brothers when I was around ten or eleven years-old. I trained there for a while and received a few junior ranks. I took up Go Ju Ryu karate a few years later and studied and trained at that for a number of years and got to black belt. At the time, the town in Scotland where I came from, Coatbridge, didn't really have any other martial arts clubs; it was karate or judo, and that was about it!

It was when I moved to Belfast that I really began studying different martial arts and tried a few different clubs; Ju-jitsu, Thai jitsu, Muay Thai, boxing and I even went back to karate for a short time. It was here that I also discovered a Wing Chun club and trained hard learning what I could whilst trying to juggle married life, three kids and a full-time job.

My path in martial arts was about to change with a chance meeting in 2008 when on holiday in Majorca. It was there I met Quan, (Tylus Quan Do), the founder of CCU (Core Combat Unlimited). He was teaching self-defence lessons around the holiday hotels and advertising himself as a third generation Bruce Lee student. I did two lessons with Quan at the hotel where we were staying, we became friends and I invited him over to Belfast to teach a seminar. A few seminars and a few more visits later, he asked me to be his first trainee instructor in CCU. I accept this challenge straight-away and soon after set up my first club which, at the beginning, I called Core Combat Unlimited Belfast, but I changed the name recently to coincide with the philosophy of what I teach, although I'm still associated to the Core Combat Unlimited family!

So what do I teach? Well I don't teach full systems or styles; I never use these two words to describe what I teach, as it only sets things in stone and that's not what I'm about. The name of my club is Concept Martial Arts Academy Belfast - the first name says it all: Concept - an idea, or a way with no way. I base it on the JKD philosophy; "Using no way as way / using what is useful and disregarding what is useless." I also use a grading system of certified levels; we tend to stay away from the traditional belt system. But I'm always changing the structure and syllabus of what I teach, as I find new ideas or concepts that fit in with what we do. My first rule though, when I'm teaching a class or if I'm teaching private lessons or teaching a self-defence seminar, is always the same and very simple - and I do think that most self-defence teachers and true martial artists would agree - "Learn not to fight! But train hard should you need to." A total different mind-set to today's UFC when I think sometimes pride and ego play a big part.

The list of my arts I take from and teach are: boxing, Wing Chun, Jkd, Kali, Silat, Muay Thai and judo. These are the main arts I'm qualified to teach, but I study and learn and teach wherever I can. I also teach yoga and use this for cool-downs at the end of a lesson. Also, I have regular guest instructors from karate, Ju-jitsu, kick-boxing, Tae Kwon Do, combat Sambo, Shooto and BJJ, and I'm always eager to learn myself, and teach students new ideas from other arts. Usually you can find interesting ideas and techniques form seminars, or just cross-training with other clubs or instructors. With today's technology even Facebook and YouTube can be a fantastic source in finding new training and teaching material. I even give students from different clubs an opportunity to demonstrate their techniques to me and my students; I'm never about staying still, always learning, growing and willing to change and adapt.

Before I teach a class, I put a lot of emphasis on conditioning and fitness. Every warm-up is different; I'd use basic running, light sparring, various stretching routines, press-ups , sit-ups, etc. I'll also use warm-up exercises from different arts. I like to always change the warm-up so students never know what to expect at each class. Conditioning the body is also a big part of the warm-ups. We hit bone against bone, punch and kick the body, slap the forearms, etc., each drill is to condition the body for taking blows and deflecting attacks. The self-defence techniques are taught usually in the second part of a class after we do the warm-up and cover basic strikes and pad work.

Sparring is another main factor of a normal class. Here students can try the techniques they have been training in that night, or try something else they may have picked up and then see how they can make it work in a simulated fight scenario. The 'Ring of Death' is a sparring type drill I like using involving one student standing in the middle of a ring of other students, the student in the middle then gets attacked by one attacker at a time, then at various and random times and angles by two or more attackers, to see their response. Controlled fun, but the drill teaches valuable lessons as you may not always be in a situation having to defend yourself against just one attacker.

It's useful using various martial arts in different classes or self-defence lessons, as some students get some techniques better than others, and so in this way everyone gets an opportunity to learn and develop. Plus it stops classes being repetitive and gives students a good variety of the arts over the following weeks and months. When they practice a new technique they are encouraged to interpret the technique on how they feel, and then finish with their own ending; it can be a choke, a take-down or more strikes using any other style or art they choose, or combine it with another technique. I leave it up to the student to feel and react and not by not over-thinking. A good example would be using the Muay Thai Teep or push kick, to keep distance from an attacker, then switching to Tae Kwon Do or karate to get up close, then using the trapping skills of Wing Chun / JKD, then follow with a take-down or throw from Ju-jitsu / judo, then some ground work from Shooto or Silat. It doesn't matter what you use or what order you use it in, as long as it works. Just go with the flow or "be like water!" as Bruce Lee would say! Not everyone can kick high, not everyone can grasp the fluid motions of some arts, not everyone can move around on the ground with ease; we are all different. I always tell the students; "I can't move exactly like you and you can't move and be exactly like me and therefore your technique, although similar, will always be different to some degree than me or anyone else." You could say I teach and encourage students to find themselves and their own way.

I only use two weapons in training; the kali /rattan stick and knife. These are the two weapons that you are most likely to come across on the streets - I haven't, as yet, come across an attacker on the streets with a nunchaku, Katana, or three-sectional staff! Knives can vary in size and shape of course, and a stick could also be a snooker cue, tree branch, walking stick, umbrella, etc., but learning how to use them can also help you understand how to defend against them. We teach twenty-eight striking angles for stick and knife. These angles are drilled religiously, so students know when called upon, they can demonstrate and defend. However, if attacked you may not always be successful of course, and anyone who teaches a knife or stick defence technique and says that it will definitely work in real life is a fool - most knife and stick attacks happen so fast and usually from behind and are very difficult, if not impossible to counter but, as Dan Inosanto (a Filipino-American martial arts instructor from California who is best known as a teacher and a student of Bruce Lee and a renowned authority on Jeet Kune Do and Filipino Martial Arts) told us at one of his seminars; "The techniques you learn may work for you but sometimes they may not work in a real-life situation! But It's best to know something, than to know nothing."

I would never have thought that, when I first started training in judo way back in 1973, I would one day be teaching my own concept of the martial arts, let alone tracing my certified martial arts linage back to Bruce Lee - my inspiration and my childhood hero. This is due to the Worldwide CCU Association, and our founder and Chief Instructor Quan, who is now a certified instructor directly under Guro Dan Inosanto.

I'm also very proud to teach the students I have at my classes and private lessons, and hope that I give them inspiration to grow and maybe become teachers themselves one day. But most importantly, I hope that they can defend themselves or their loved ones if they ever find themselves in a bad situation. At Concept, I personally believe that training and researching as many of the martial arts as possible which is so important to growing and learning. You may favour one style or one system over another, but try everything and don't be closed-minded. It doesn't matter which art you take from as long as it works for you and when you need it to work for you.

You are the art!

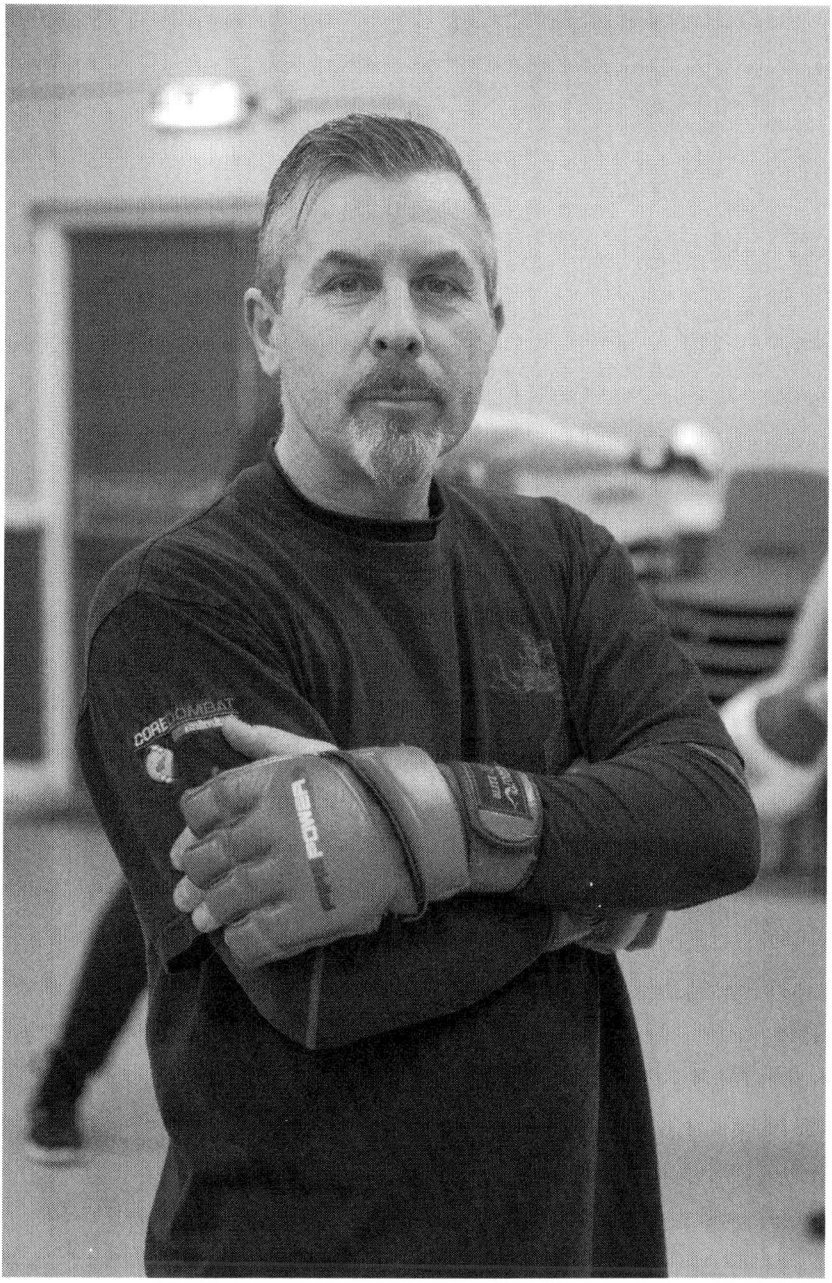
CORE COMBAT
POWER

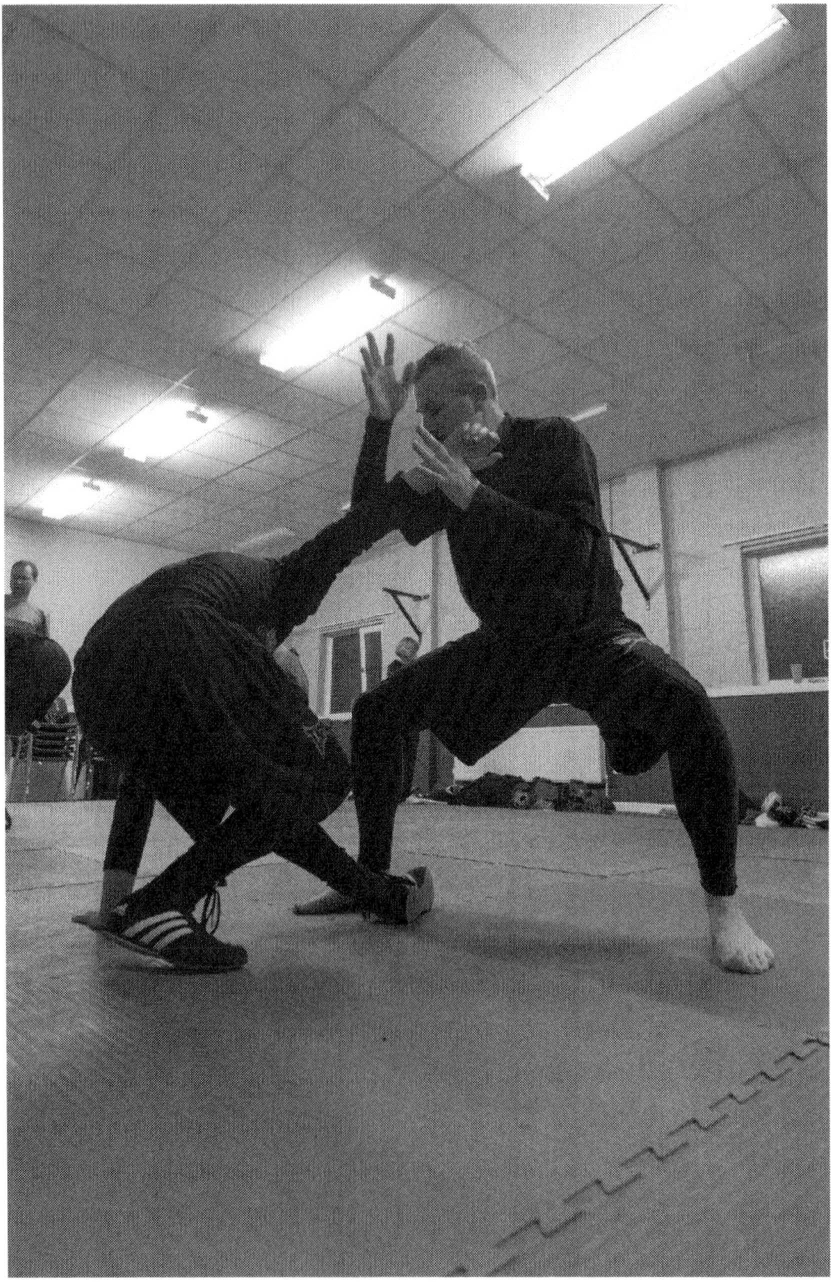

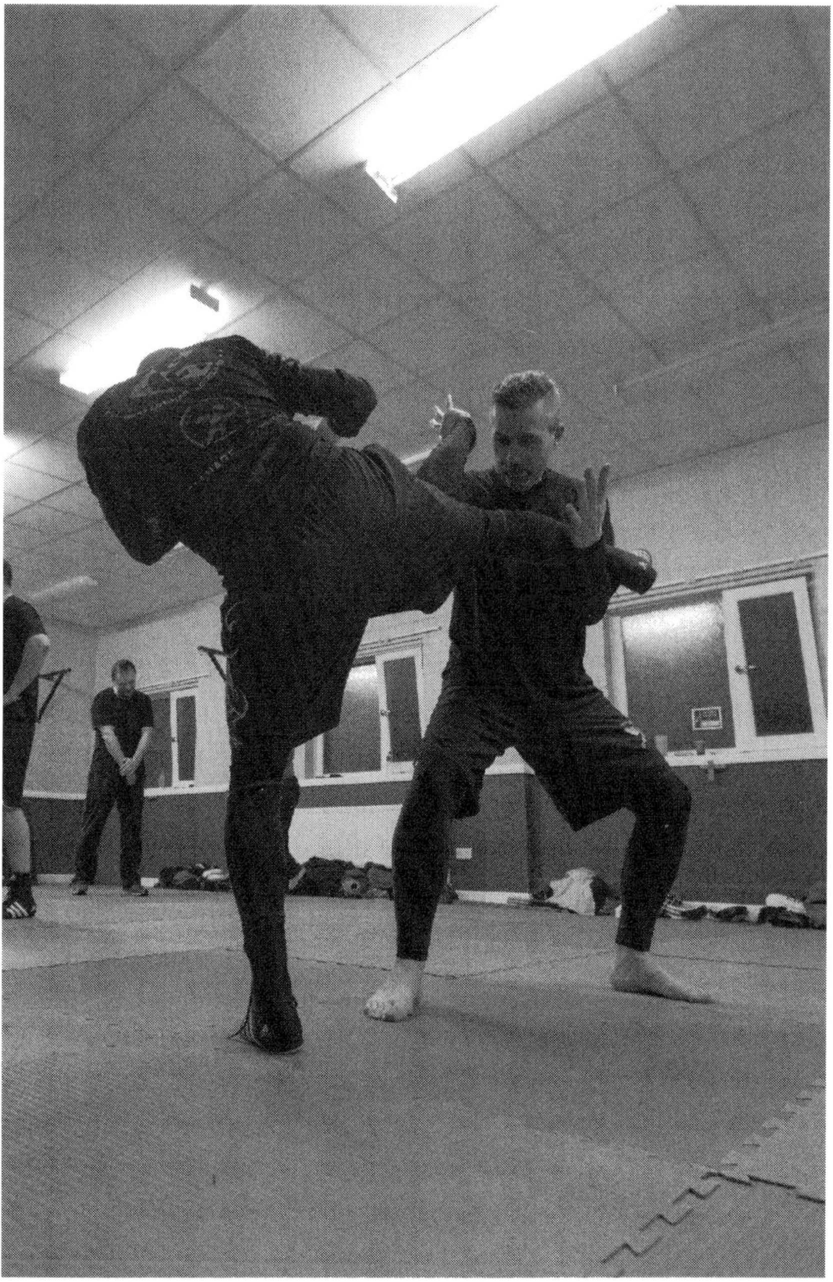

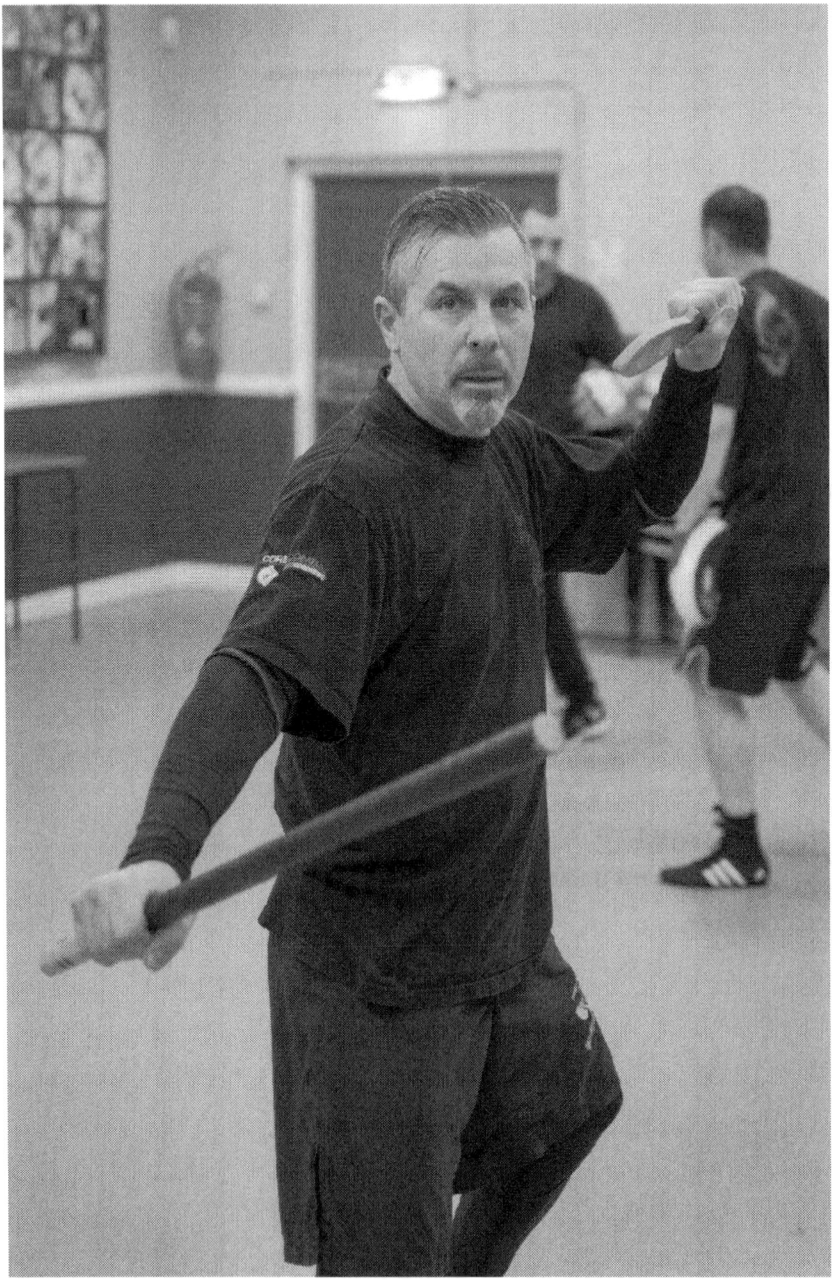

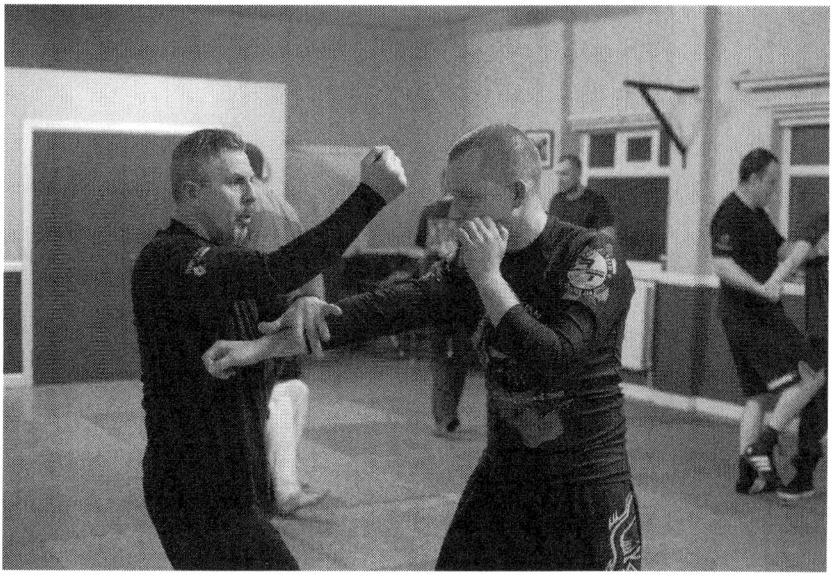

ETIQUETTE CLOSE QUARTER COMBAT & CONTROL - Anything Considered, Everything Measured

By Benji Churchill

Etiquette Close Quarter Combat & Control is a comprehensive, yet simple and effective true, full and real self defence system.

It covers every element of self-protection. Our training also includes knowledge of the law, by legally competent professionals, victim profiles, the science psychology of combat, physiology, positive mind-set and functional ability. The objective is to equip our private security operatives with regular training that allows them to practice and enhance their skills and knowledge. This has also lead to providing self-defence to the public and persons specially invited to our regular sessions.

I have a background from several martial arts including Hapkido, Ju-jutsu and Taiho Jutsu, amongst others, and at the time found Taiho Jutsu the perfect martial art for the professional role I and my security firm take on. However, the breakthrough came when I attended Professional Instructor training. It was in front of me all along but the opposite of what is all too common drilled into people involved in martial arts: It was in recognising the science of combat. Along with my new mind-set which made me see what was good from my martial arts background, and what wasn't, was a way to train, so it actually became effective in the real world and which also fitted into the exact needs of our security operatives. I also completed training in various other systems of simple close quarter combat, which has really enabled me to fine tune the Etiquette system.

Combat / Self Defence

In our system anything is considered but everything has to be measured against the questions / principles that are of the core of our training and the Etiquette system.

The objective of the system is to be as safe as possible, whilst having the minimum amount of components / skills in order to train to maximum effect of those components / skills. Once the key skills are completely mastered, the whole system then introduces some more obscure skills for self-defence and street combat to counter any

Primitive Stress Response, or 'fight or flight' a person may experience when in a situation causing a significantly high emotional state.

Weapons Defence

Weapon defence and weapon use in training can be a controversial one, but essential, and it's almost certainly better to have some form of training than none at all. If attacked with a weapon the predicament you are in is undeniably very dangerous and defending yourself against such an attacker is not a simple task: there is no text-book answer.

The Etiquette system uses exactly the same moves and principles for unarmed as armed, just slight tweaks and adaptations to the application and result. However, we focus proportionately on this in our training, for example the chances are being threatened by a person with a gun is extremely low compared to knives and blunt-edged weapons, so therefore our training is representative of the risk. Our weapon training involves ASP, baton and Kubaton training, as well as advanced techniques involving several different blades, as well as everyday objects that can – and often are – turned into weapons.

Control

The control element is also included in the overall system due to the nature of its origin and development, and is designed and used by operatives in the company who require physical skills to defend themselves as well as to arrest, control or restrain others. Including in the training is simple transportation locks, to C-Clamp manoeuvrers.

Handcuffing

Also included in the whole system is the use of handcuffs and how handcuffs can be used as self-defence, again because of the purpose in the creation of the Etiquette system particularly for use within the security industry.

Fighting, Without Fighting

We, as humans, give out a frequency and pick up on frequencies. This is very important to understand. Understanding how to tune in on bad vibrations, how to recognise strategies and behaviour in order to avoid a possible situation, or how make a pre-emptive strike in terms of how you hold yourself, what you say, how you say it is and the way you say it, is vitally important. Fighting without fighting should really be fighting mentally! Presenting yourself as assertive as opposed to aggressive, walking proud and confident, displaying good posture and balance; body language is key to winning most fights... without even fighting.

Law

Self-defence is often often too focussed on physically protecting ourselves, and not on the whole approach; training physically, mentally and legally. So Etiquette's training is in tandem with the knowledge that is necessary to learn in order to operate effectively within the law, things like knowing that you're allowed to make a pre-emptive strike to ensure your safety when you honestly and instinctively believed it to be necessary and proportionate to the risk. This basic understanding of the law removes doubt, and removing doubt gives us confidence and makes us perform more effectively. And being effective is the name of the game in combat.

Training

the way our senior instructors construct sessions, and their teaching techniques are vital in the ability for those learning to perform effectively in real life. The warm-up has its place to help reduce injury, but also to tire out the body, so if you can complete training when your body is exhausted, this is pivotal in getting a little better and real development. Being fitter, stronger, quicker are all bonuses too, so with that in mind, the warm-up is also body conditioning to achieve those ends. Functional bodyweight movements are the staple approach in warm-ups, but special program objectives and methods can vary and include team log PT, obstacle courses, weights and endurance training.

Drilling skills is also an important aspect, ingraining skills into muscle memory in order to make them instinctive. What makes the difference is the ability to perform under pressure, when the primitive stress response is kicking in. This is where skills learnt need to be tested and ingrained, and is the real core of our training.

Application

Obviously the most import objective of self-defence training is to defend yourself in violent and aggressive situations, and deal with them effectively. Further objectives in this system are to keep safe and to effectively work and operate in several professional roles. Also, notably to protect others (in close protection), and certain assets (in asset protection). In addition there is the element of arresting / controlling an individual too.

Looking Forward

Looking forward, and to the development of this system, Etiquette is definitely something people are going to hear about in the future, especially within the security sector that make up the majority of our learners. It's certainly not developed to its full potential yet either, with instructional book and a DVD series planned, you will be hearing a lot more about Etiquette Close Quarter Combat & Control.

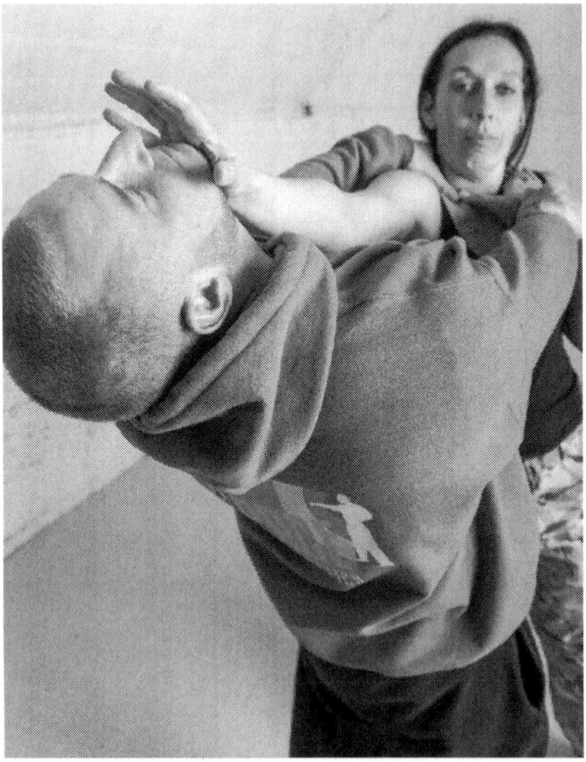

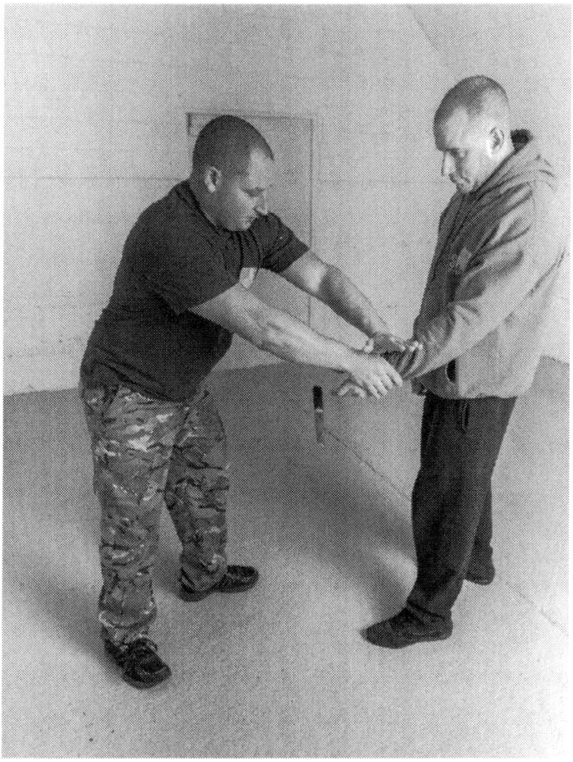

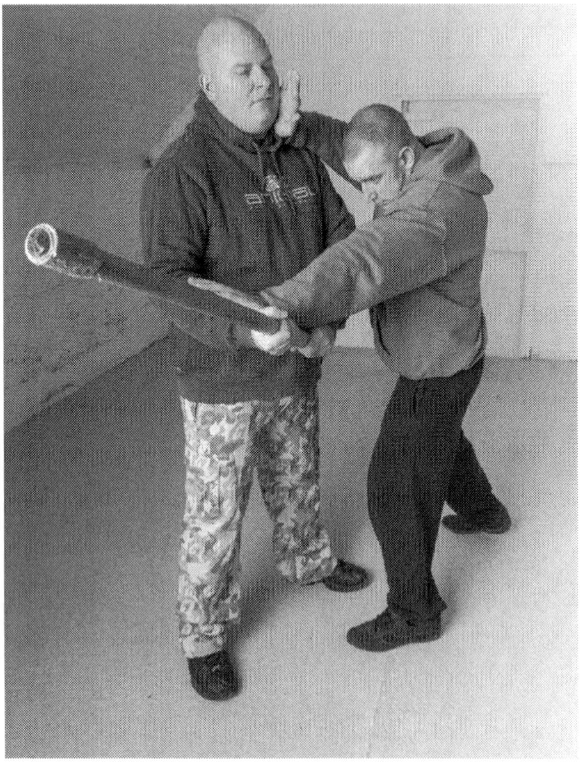

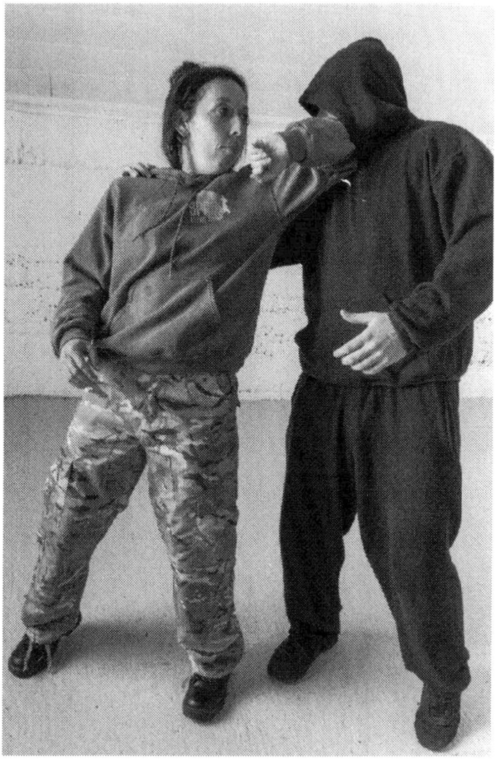

ESCRIMA CONCEPTS - A Weapon to Unarmed System

By Steve Tappin

The Escrima Concepts organisation was founded by me, with the support of my family and friends. It is a weapon-to-unarmed system, designed to cope with potentially harmful conflicts, due to an ever-increasing violent society. Many martial arts teach their students unarmed combat for years, and then teach their students to train with weapons, but we teach them both from day one. Our system was designed because myself and the majority of my senior instructors were raised in the reality of life; we worked the doors, and we understood the street where people had an 'end them' mentality, a slap was never enough, they wanted respect and for you to fear them.

At the same time, we had a common interest in martial arts and so we came together from all parts of the world to prepare our members for our way of training, with the advantage of a street mentality, combined with our own personal experiences when dealing with violence. This gave us an insight into teaching honestly without the fancy techniques. We have been called aggressive, but we fight to protect others. We are educators, and our aim is to make our students better, bring them out of their comfort zones, help them gain confidence and a sense of achievement but, more importantly, to learn within a social environment. We don't want our students going through the painful and mental barriers of a violent lifestyle we instructors have had, but we do want them to accept that we have taken something that's often bad in society and used it to help people be environmentally prepared, and better equipped if violence does ever enter their world. We are time savers too; what took us years to learn benefits our students in a fraction of the time. We are against violence, but we understand it, and so we teach our system honestly for the fight that we hope would never happen. We teach an energetic, intelligent system without the pain, because the people that need our help the most, rarely return if they get constantly get hurt. We are not a macho-egotistical system either; we teach with the benefit of our experiences which has included teaching many streetwise instructors from other systems too. Many of us from violence turn against violence and so our teachings reflect the street mentality without glorifying it to our students.

Many phrases come to mind when describing various combat

systems; urban, reality, dirty fighting, street and street-wise training, but many instructors have not served their time on the streets, nor fought with people intent on doing them real harm; it's a different world and a very different mentality out there. Of course, it does not mean they cannot teach, or that they cannot fight, but the mental preparation for the streets is different, plus you never really find out what you can do, or are prepared to do, and then learn to deal with it emotionally until you are put in that position and then having to deal with the consequences. The world is full of conflict, and with weapon attacks happening every day, we need to be environmentally alert and prepared to deal with all types of emergencies in everyday life.

Very few martial arts actually train and spar efficiently with weapons; some approach weapons training from their unarmed perspective, others do singular attacks so the defender can get a specific technique mastered, others do endless rehearsed flow drills; we have seen this type of training so many times but often the intent and attitude is lacking or non-existent, and very few actually use weapons correctly, or attack correctly, using all the tools (feet, hands, elbows, knees or head) in different combinations. We build our students up from simple attacks to random, unknown, powerful and fast attacks, and multiple attacks and in any combination, at any angle.

We teach a complete stand-alone armed and unarmed system based on the needs of an ever-demanding society. Although I've been involved with Escrima since the '70s, our own system of Escrima Concepts began in 2003 and we teach regularly in eleven countries and last year awarded our first females to instructor status. We train hard but it should be fun too.

Being a conceptual system based on all my years teaching and observations, weapon training, real-life experiences and unarmed training, our aim is to help individuals to self-discover and, as students learn and understand more, they can adapt their training to suit their personal needs; we do not want clones copying teachers, we want each person to get the most out of training for themselves. To enable our students to progress, we have a syllabus that covers the many basics that enable us to highlight our concepts to prepare for reality training. Preparing those that train with us for the real world means - from the very first time students begin to train - teaching how to train and combine together body mechanics and weapon mechanics, as well as mental preparation, knowing your angles and learning about pressure, understanding positioning and targeting, and the consequences of your actions. The years of training with different weapons became the backbone of our teaching, it had to be because people do fight with weapons and always have. We have an intelligent system, often considered by others as an aggressive system, but a system that has removed the showy techniques and tricks that create bad habits that can leave you untrained for a real-life threats.

We train for minimum force, control and the law of the land right through to life-threatening situations. We learn to control the space in order to improve contact. Whether we fight unarmed or armed, our mind-set is the same; we always assume our opponents are potentially armed because unfortunately that is the nature of the streets. No teacher can guarantee survival against dangerous attacks with weapons (or unarmed attacks) but with honest effective training and the correct mental preparation, and pressure-testing, we hope to increase your chances of survival.

If the criteria of a reality based system consists of real experiences of violent encounters, with many years of martial arts, alongside the right mental attitude that allows us to train our students physically with mental preparation, safely, without glorifying violence, then we are that reality based system.

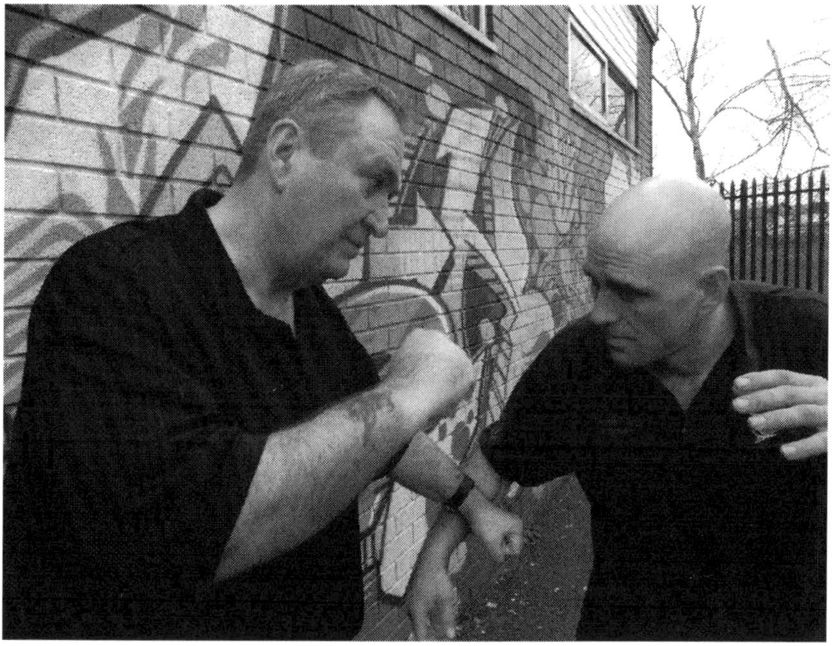

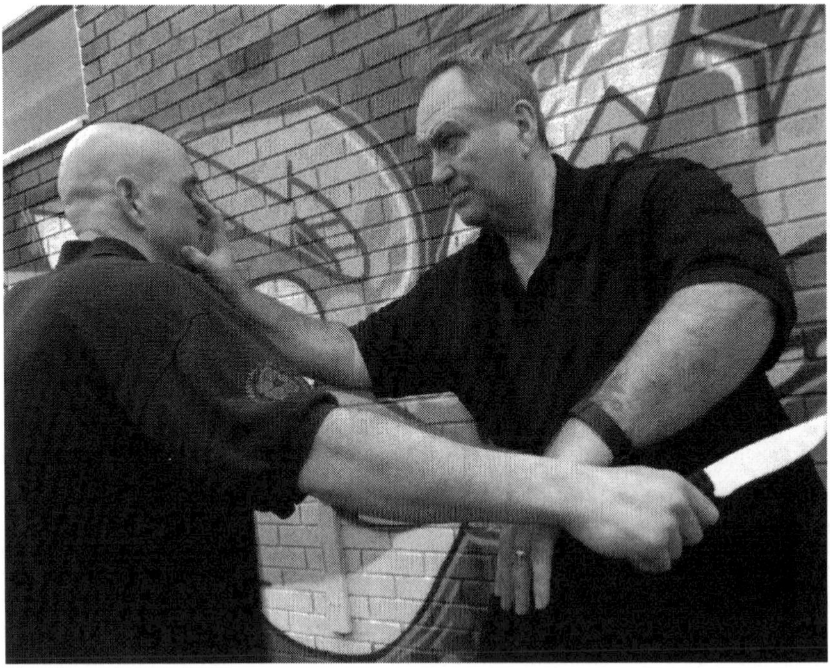

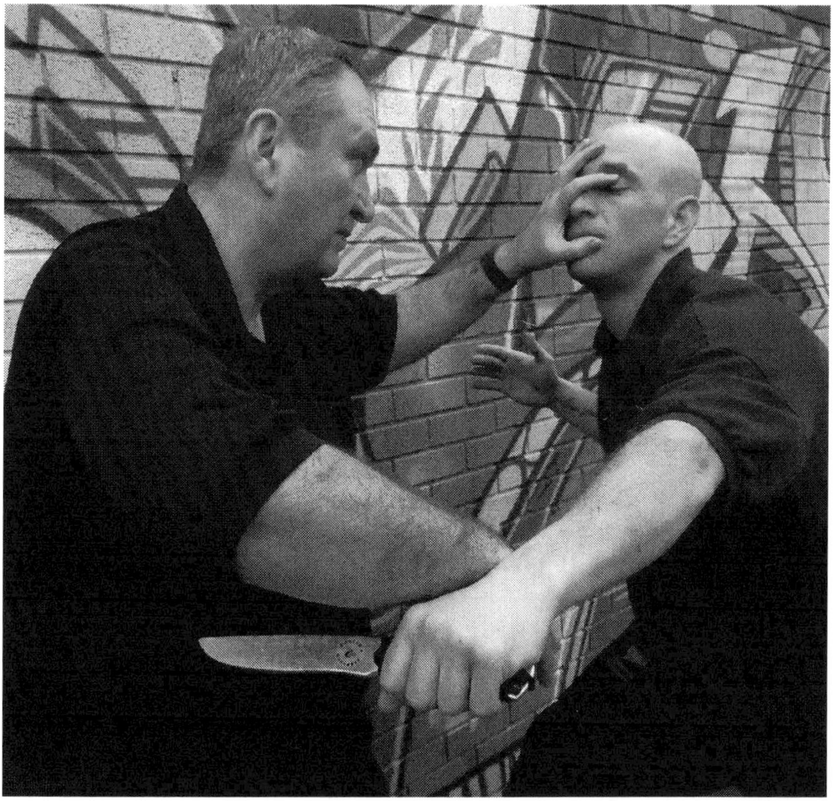

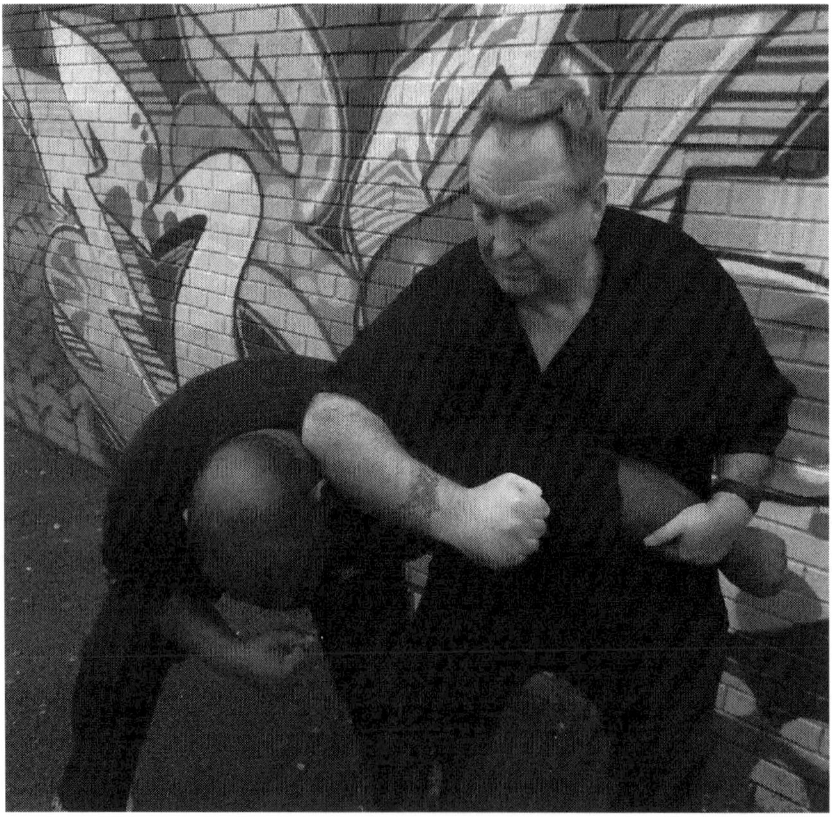

FIGHT FORTRESS - Keeping it Simple and Effective
By Simon Morrell

As a victim of bullies and violent people, for many years I looked for salvation and, like many before me, found it in martial arts, namely Shotokan karate. The club I trained at was a tough, Japanese style regime and at times I struggled to hold my bottle, but I did - gaining advance grade at the age of just eighteen.

However, like those that went before me, I left my training by the wayside as pubs and girls beckoned. I was to return some years later to a local Shukokai club and W.C.K.A. kickboxing club. I absolutely loved the heavy sparring and took to competing, but even though I harboured no desire to teach (I felt I was too young and without the required experience), on some level I realised that one system / style did not hold all the answers I was looking for.

I wanted something that could address traditional martial arts, competition, sparring and confidence building, and that could teach me to hold my own in a real time. I wanted a reality based system.

At this time I was introduced to Western boxing and, at just under nine stone, sparred on a regular basis with a professional heavyweight who pulled no punches. It was at this gym that I discovered hand skills and speed more akin to what I was looking for, but more importantly the regular sessions made me realise I did indeed have 'bottle.'

Little did I know at the time that this diversity in training (although they were all striking systems) would eventually form the nucleus of the Fight Fortress syllabus, but still something was missing and it was only whilst training for my 1st dan black belt under Alfie 'The Animal' Lewis (who, to this day, twenty-five years later, remains my Sensei and friend) that I happened across Geoff Thompson.

Geoff and I hit it off immediately, and once a month I started making long trips to Coventry to train all day on British Combat Association Instructor's courses. It was during these trips that I realised what the missing pieces were that would make my system 'fit for purpose.'

Quite simply, the pieces were short range or Close Quarter Combat, and by that I include close-in strikes (elbows, knees, head-butts) and grappling. With the help of some great instructors including the well-known Peter Consterdine, I started to develop a syllabus that could take in my 3rd dan test (having already fought two European Vale Tudo Champions over ten full contact rounds for my 2nd dan. *Note: Vale Tudo was the original name for all out, no-holds-barred fighting, pretty much cage fighting now*). The same syllabus would filter all the way down to yellow belt, our first grading.

I was starting to establish myself as a well known instructor and so furthered my education by training on the first ever UK Krav Maga seminar under Eyal Yanilov. I believe Eyal Yanliov was one of the first instructors to bring Krav Maga to the UK, and the first Krav Maga instructor I trained under at a British Combat Association seminar in Coventry, roughly twenty years ago. I also attended the Salford Wrestling Academy under Mr. Matt Clempner. Matt was a serving police officer in Manchester and ran seminars at the Academy. I attended Russian Close Quarter Combat seminar with him there and, despite it being a tough, pretty brutal day, came away with a very healthy respect for both Mr. Clempner and his system.

All this training, usually under very stressful levels, made me realise I was also developing a very important, much ignored skill; Fear Control, something I was later to be declared an authority on by Geoff Thompson.

Slowly, and sometimes without me realising it, the Fight Fortress syllabus developed and it is something that continues to do so today and every day. We try and improve and evolve with every session.

Nowadays the self protection side of our training ethos largely follows the Krav Maga mindset of training, something we refer to as the three second fight: hit first, hit hard and get out! Pre-emptive strikes are encouraged, but under the right circumstances in law. It is common knowledge with instructors (or it certainly should be) that if we have honest belief we are about to be attacked, then we can hit first with reasonable force, and I relay that to my students, but that is as far as I go in addressing the legal issues.

The law both interests and fascinates me and in the past I have allowed myself to get dragged into long-winded debates such as; "Would a jury see it that way?" or "what would my sentence be if found guilty?" or "would I even get charged?" etc., etc. These questions, and many more, are regularly put to me by my students wanting to know every detail of every potential conflict. Certainly we have a duty to educate students on consequence of using their skills in a street combat situation, but only to a point - otherwise we become a debating society and not a combat training group! And so I quickly address the issues with the two main statements; "honest belief," and "justifiable force," before moving on. If a student wants more than that they can go online to research more detail for themselves.

I'm a big believer in fitness playing a big part in training, but again it has to be fit for purpose. Each session starts with Battle Fit which is a twenty minute non-stop blast of drills relative to fighting. We are not a fitness club; all that we do is geared toward combat.

Our training is split into two entities; one concentrates on sport, primarily kickboxing. The sessions for this side of our training is very specific; we train two minute rounds - two minutes running, two minutes bag work, two minutes pad work, two minutes sparring etc., all simulating an actual bout time. Sparring is heavy but controlled, as I have found too much heavy sparring is counter productive to longevity and we quickly end up saying 'goodbye' to a fair number of students.

However the mainstay of Fight Fortress and the classes that by far attracts the most students, is our reality based training, drawing from Krav Maga, practical karate, Olympic wrestling and Western boxing.

Controlling your opponent's distance is an absolute must before we can even think about a physical reaction, strike etc. I teach students to have their hands up high (no fists, open hands) with their strongest hand to the rear to maximise power should a strike become inevitable. Our training also extensively covers escapes from holds; choke, strangle, bear-hug, head-lock and others, and the first thing a student is taught is to simultaneously base and make breathing space - by base I mean make a solid stance by dropping your strongest leg back and keeping your body weight low. It is quite easy to control pick up an opponent whose centre of gravity is high. Think of it like a stick in the wind compared to a rock on the ground.

As for preference the techniques used in an attack? Again this will boil down to experience, mental attitude and of course any natural ability the combative may posses, but before striking, I encourage verbal discussion but if it (the conflict) has gone beyond this point, then the power of your strike should not be considered; some years ago I remember reading that in legal proceedings a judge ruled: "A person does not have to weigh the niceties of their punch when it comes to the matter of self-defence." In other words; we don't not need to, nor do we have time to consider our weight, power, fitness and experience against an assailant; there simply isn't enough time, moreover, it is likely that we have no clue as to the attackers' skills, experience and background either. All we know is that there is a risk and we have no clue as to how big that risk is. It was once said there are two types of risk; High risk and unknown risk. Never low risk.

Combat can be a complicated business but keeping it simple is usually the most effective way.

Simon Morrell's
KRAV MAGA
KICKBOXING
@
GHT FORTRE
www.simonmorrell.com

Simon Morrell's
KRAV MAGA
KICKBOXING
@
FIGHT FORTRE
www.simonmorrell.com
勇
忠
希

Simon Morrell's
KRAV MAGA
KICKBOXING
@
FIGHT FORT
www.simonmorrell.co

HARD TARGET COMBAT SYSTEM - Practical Approaches to Aggressive Engagements
By Mo Teague

My martial arts journey began in 1971 when I started training in judo and Shotokan karate, grading under the legendary Japanese karate master Keinosuke Endoeda. Throughout the years I have sought out the best instructors and practitioners to learn and draw inspiration from, including Austin Goh, Victor Kan, Rick Young, Rick Faye, Erik Paulson, Geoff Thompson, Peter Consterdine, Tommy Thompson, Dan Inosanto, Carlson Gracie and of course my teacher and main inspiration Grand Master Richard Bustillo. Much of this training was seminar based, but it was enough to draw ideas, concepts and inspiration from to add to my ever evolving knowledge, skill-set and real world experience to form the Hard Target Combat System; Itself an ever evolving process and work in progress.

I served for fifteen years in an elite regiment of the British Army. After which I worked for over ten years as a bouncer, many of those years I worked on my own in a biker bar, no one else would work there. I survived over three hundred fights, as much by luck as skill, but learned many valuable lessons along the way; they say pain is a great teacher! I have trained literally thousands of students world-wide including military, law enforcement, close protection and security personnel and, as importantly, school children and housewives in the HTCS. I have aspiration to excellence in all things and an expectation of others to aspire to the same.

The Hard Target Combat System (HTCS) is a modern integrated combatives system characterised by a relevant and practical approach to aggressive and violent engagements that enables practitioners to achieve a high level of proficiency within a relatively short period of instruction and training. The system is based on combat tested and proven principles, procedures and tactical concepts, rather than specific techniques *per se*; this is an important distinction because systems that are technique driven do not allow for the various confrontation attack scenarios that occur in a modern violent encounter.

Through the integration of proven principles, procedures, tactical concepts and relevant techniques taught by highly qualified and experienced instructors utilising accelerated learning teaching methods, the HTCS is recognised as one of the most relevant, efficient combat systems in the world today.

Harm's Way

To those who go into 'harms way,' the 'quiet professionals,' violence is not an abstract notion but accepted as a reality, and consequence of service and sacrifice to country, community, family and others they serve to protect. The levels of violence faced by the quiet professionals' demands a level of performance in training, on operations, and in tactical and techniques application that can only be acquired by thoughtful process, good solid instruction, and damn hard work.

The Quiet Professionals

The quiet professionals are the military and law enforcement personnel, close protection officers, corrections officers, security and other blue-light sheepdog professionals.

First responders who operate at the interface between those who live by a different code, alien and counter to that which society observes, abides and functions, and those who are their targets and victims. Terrorists, criminals and enemy soldiers bring a level of violence that can be contained, countered and defeated only by those who are better trained, more motivated and committed, and who act with just cause and moral certitude in the name of justice and humanity... The Quiet Professionals.

Categories Of Violence

The HTCS addresses all categories of violence including:

- Social
- Criminal
- Terrorist
- Political
- Warfare

These categories all have subcategories, for example warfare / soldiers on peacekeeping / observer duties require different / additional skill-sets to soldiers involved in full scale nation v nation conflict. Likewise a police patrol officer, requires a different / additional skill-set be they tactical or technical to an armed response officer. Ultimately regardless of context it comes down to face to face, hand to hand, hand to weapon tactical engagement scenarios.

HTCS Skill-Set

When delivering a training package, there are a number of factors to consider in determining the skill-set to be taught.

- Operational Role
- Use of Force Policies, Rules of Engagement
- Operational Procedures
- Public Relations / Image
- Current Standard of Student Motivation
- Support and Resources
- Number of Students
- Culture and Politics
- Standards and Levels of Performance
- Objectives

This is not the full list and in bullet point only but, as you can see, it's much more than a list of techniques with no context that you see in most articles. Teaching techniques is the easy part; I recently had to teach a security guard force in a politically and culturally sensitive environment, where the students' English language was poor and motivation to learn low, and for them to be able to demonstrate a forty-technique skill-set that went from escort techniques up to lethal use of force techniques, whilst adhering to all Health & Safety protocols and use of force policies, in under forty hours of training which included fitness training. All standards were achieved with a 98% pass rate of students.

As well as techniques, other supporting information must be taught including:

- Tactics
- Decision making
- Mind-set
- Awareness
- Deployment of weapons and Resources
- Tactical Communication

Again this is not a full list and in bullet points only. Although I have explained in overview the HTCS in context to the Quiet Professionals, it can be modified and tailored through strategic planning to suit all those who face violence on a daily basis.

I have seen death and destruction; I have faced death and taken lives in defence of my own and others. I know the value of life and love, and I am passionate about teaching others how to stay alive when going into harm's way.

The HTCS is the result of my own experiences, research study and training. It is ever evolving and improving to counter and defeat the increasing level of threats and violence we all face on a daily basis perpetuated by evil men.

I've learned some good lessons along the way...

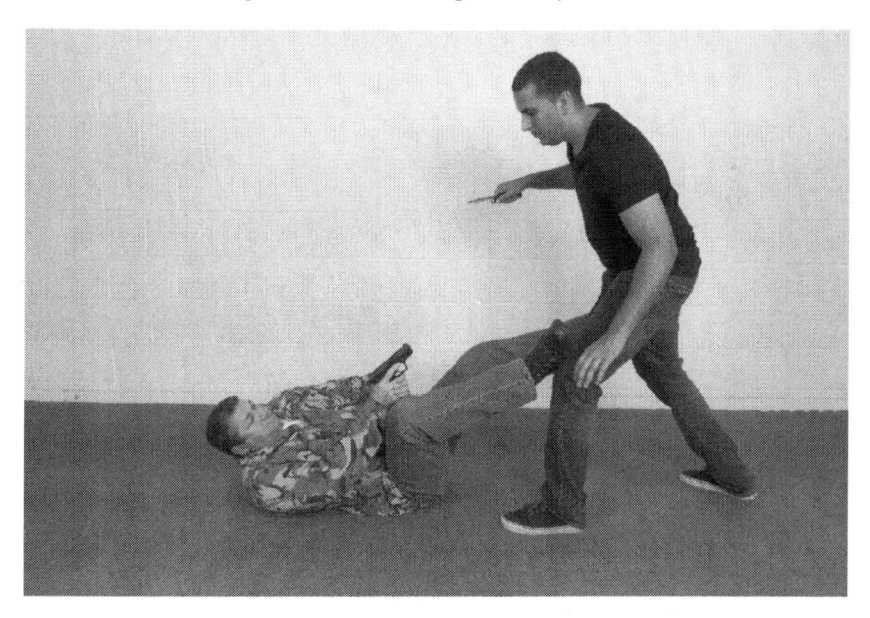

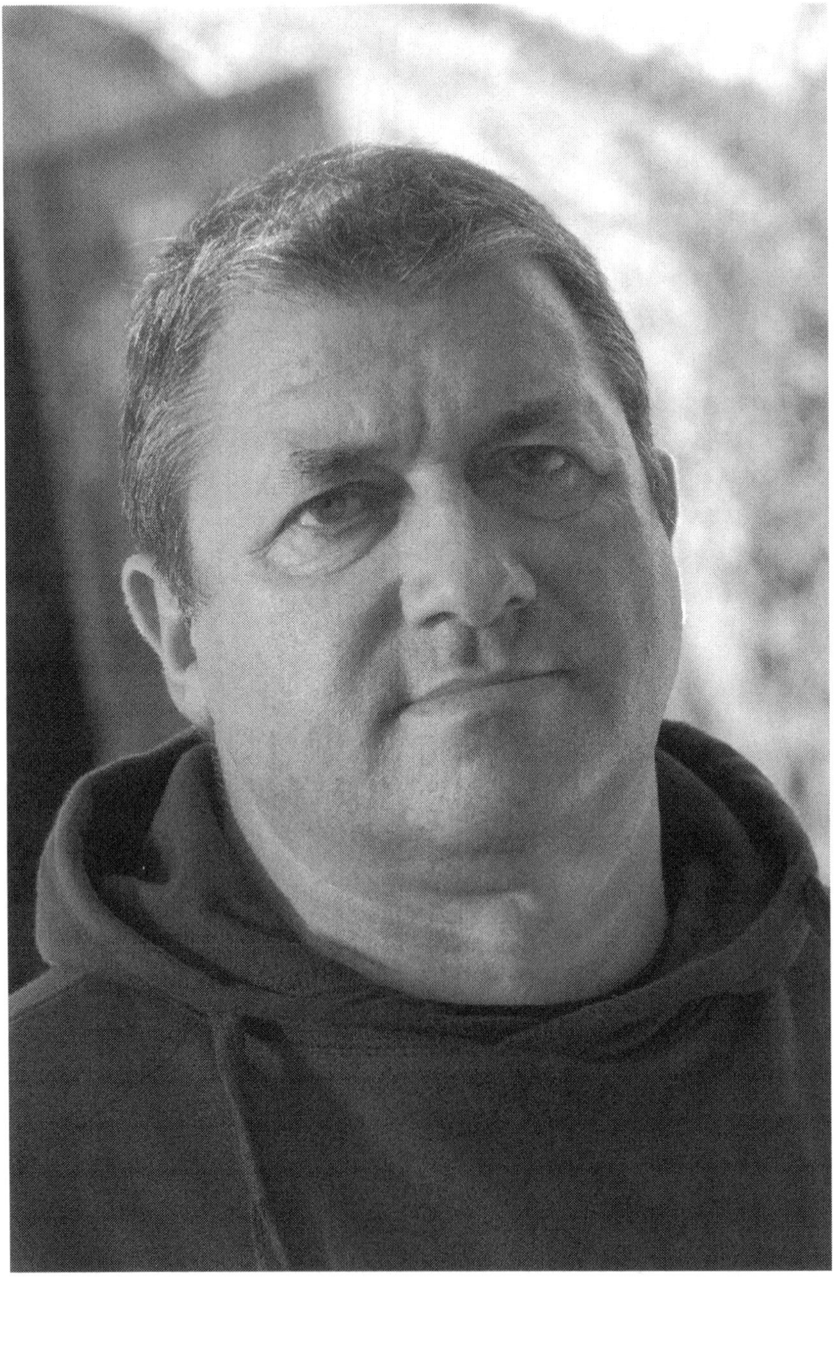

ISRAELI KRAV MAGA – Globally Recognized for its Simplicity and Brutal Efficiency
By David Kahn - USA

The Israeli Krav Maga Advantage

The Israeli Krav Maga self-defence system has achieved global recognition for its efficiency, simplicity and, when required, brutal efficiency. Krav Maga's world-renowned tactics were originally developed for a modern army, the Israel Defense Force (IDF), as its official self-defence and close-quarters-combat system. Krav Maga is usually translated as 'contact combat.' This specific translation is significant because of the word 'combat,' rather than the word 'fight.' Combat is considered a life and death situation devoid of any sporting element, chivalry, or rules. This differentiation is fundamental to Krav Maga's methods and philosophy.

Responsible people pursue Krav Maga training to shield themselves from violence; not to orchestrate violence. Krav Maga founder Imi Lichtenfeld designed Krav Maga for people of all shapes, sizes, ages, and physical abilities. Krav Maga's fundamental principles were developed by Imi to protect the pre-war Jewish community in Slovakia. Imi understood that actual violence differs greatly from choreographed training, and adopted his tactics accordingly. Most important, Krav Maga develops a paramount fighting, no-quit attitude. A few instinctive Krav Maga tactics enable you to survive the most common onslaughts.

My Introduction To Krav Maga

My introduction to Israeli Krav Maga floored me... literally. During the first week of law school, I met Israeli Krav Maga Association (IKMA) senior instructor Rick Blitstein. During my first class, Rick decided to use me as a would-be assailant. I didn't remember feeling particularly vulnerable; After my college football career ended, I continued my strength and conditioning program and stood 5' 11" tall and weighed about two hundred pounds. Rick, who was about three inches shorter and about forty pounds lighter, was certainly fit, but if you saw both of us on the street and knew nothing of our background, you probably would have bet that I could easily take Rick in a confrontation.

Rick asked me to come at him. The next thing I remember after he grabbed my wrist, was that I lay on the floor. Rick was standing over me with his size eight foot on my throat. 'What just happened?' I wondered as I looked up at him in daze. He grinned down at me in a knowing manner – obviously, I was not the first. I continued to train intensively with Rick privately for three years. Rick then sent me to train with Grandmaster Haim Gidon of the Israeli Krav Maga Organization (Gidon System). And to date I have trained extensively with Grandmaster Gidon in excess of three dozen times.

The Israeli Krav Maga Association (Gidon System)

The IKMA is Krav Maga founder Imi Lichtenfeld's original Krav Maga organization, and the governing body for Israeli Krav Maga recognized by the Israeli government. Haim introduced several key weapons technique modifications and improvements – all formally approved by Krav Maga founder Imi Lichtenfeld. While improving the Krav Maga system daily, Haim follows Imi's fundamental premise that Krav Maga must work for everyone, even against the most skilled adversaries. Constant enhancement, evolution and adaptability make Krav Maga a most formidable fighting method. Krav Maga's hallmark and genius is to teach anyone to successfully defend against any type of attack attacks.

Krav Maga's Overriding Philosophy: Do Whatever Works

Krav Maga's overriding philosophy is to do 'whatever works' to deliver you from harm's way. If push comes to shove, literally and figuratively, Krav Maga is designed to handle any type or kind of personal violence. Krav Maga's goal is to neutralize an attacker quickly and decisively. It is designed to thwart and neutralize any type of threat or attack with a torrent of overwhelming counter-violence. The tactics are designed as defensive capability multipliers. A few mastered Krav Maga techniques are highly effective in most situations. When properly learned and practised, these tactics become first nature.

While Krav Maga emphasizes several basic core techniques and advanced applications of these same tactics to prevail in a dangerous situation, there is no absolute or correct answer. The system's application is flexible – true to its modern combat evolution. Techniques are constantly modified, revised, added and discarded as real-life encounters are taken into account, analysed and absorbed.

By design, Krav Maga defences are specific and yet, adaptable to handle the fluidity and unpredictability of combat. In other words, general principals are applied and customized to suit the needs of a particular situation. Each defence combines deflection-redirections, evasive actions, and simultaneous or near-simultaneous counter-attacks with extreme prejudice to dominate the opponent. The defences are also designed for multiple attacker situations to shield the defender, incapacitate the attacker, and immediately confiscate any weapon for the defender's use.

In short, you'll attack the attacker. Importantly, the tactics and techniques are designed to provide the defender with a pre-emption capability prior to a weapon being deployed. The goal is not to allow an assailant to get the drop on you. Your recognition of his intent and body language literally and figuratively will allow you to cut the legs out from under him.

Krav Maga's Approach to Facing Down Unavoidable Violence: Instinctive, Aggressive Reaction Adhering to No Rules

Street violence is volatile, unpredictable and often unannounced (though there may be pre-violence indicators a victim did not recognize). Concerted, determined violence seldom lasts more than a few seconds. Regardless of an attacker's size, strength, training, or physical ability, you will prevail by delivering debilitating, overwhelming counter-violence using maximum speed and aggression. The sooner you spot a potential aggressor, the more time you will have to act. If there is no non-violent solution available, proceed with extreme prejudice until you end the violent confrontation on your terms.

The 'no rules' credo distinguishes Krav Maga self-defence from sport fighting. In a scripted sport fight the following non-exclusive tactics are generally banned: eye gouges; throat strikes; head-butting; biting; striking the spine; small joint manipulation; kidney, liver, clavicle and knee joint strikes; and slamming an attacker to the ground on the attacker's head. These are exactly the combined core tactics Krav Maga emphasizes.

If you must fight, identify the opportune moment to attack the attacker with a continuous overwhelming counter-attack using retzev or 'continuous combat motion.' Combined with simultaneous defence and attack (or near simultaneous defence and attack), retzev is a seamless, decisive, and overpowering counter-attack. In short, injury breaks down human anatomical structure and function - the aggressor's ability to harm you. When justified, administering sequential injurious physical trauma epitomizes Krav Maga counter-violence or retzev.

Legal Considerations

Never forget that the level of force you use to defend yourself must be objectively 'reasonable' to stop a threat. Once the threat is no more, you must cease counter-offensive actions. Importantly, reacting from surprise allows the use of more force because you do not have time to rationally or reasonably analyse the situation. In the aftermath of defending yourself, you'll need to articulate that you had no choice when faced with a threat who had the:

- Intent (stated or evident goal of harming you)
- Capability (has the prowess or tools to harm you)
- Opportunity (proximity)

If any of the above three criteria is absent or becomes absent or you could avoid the threat, you are no longer acting in self-defence.

Training

Imi emphasized, as does current Grandmaster Gidon, that training must attempt to simulate a real attack for you to understand the speed, ferocity, and strength a determined attacker may direct at you. The tactics must work against concerted resistance. To adopt and streamline the Krav Maga method, personalize the techniques and make them your own. Instinct assumes control to defend against a violent assault.

Conflict Avoidance & Escaping Violence

Krav Maga emphasizes common sense and that a few street smarts are your optimum weapons to avoid violence. In short, avoidance is often about keeping your cool (as is every other aspect of self-defence including de-escalation, escape and evasion and, lastly, fighting for your life.). The key to avoiding social violence is not to provide provocations. Keep in mind, that people will generally not escalate if they are unconvinced that they can 'get away' with it (i.e. avoid physical damage to themselves and escape legal prosecution).

Escape methods are a vital part of the Krav Maga curriculum. Escape is your second choice when avoidance and de-escalation fail. To escape, your goal is to evade physical contact and preserve your ability to successfully flee. Your ultimate goal is to find safety through breaking contact and losing any pursuers by quickly hiding or finding safety among other people.

Awareness Methods

Developing recognition of pre-violence indicators along with impending attacks is instrumental to Krav Maga. Situational awareness of whom and what to keenly observe is all-important and common sense should prevail. Generally, human behaviour is overwhelmingly predictable. The Israeli Krav Maga curriculum places heavy emphasis on the ability to recognize, avoid, and / or pre-empt physical conflicts. Recognition of an impending attack / threat obviously affords the greatest reaction time for the following solutions: (a) avoidance, (b) de-escalation, (c) escape and (d) counter-violence. Always trust your instincts and intuition. A large part of awareness is to understand your capacity and limits. In other words, what verbal or physical abuse you might accept or what actions will cross your proverbial 'Red Line.'

Recognizing Hostile Body Language and Pre-conflict Kinesic Indicators

When facing street violence, you can usually recognize verbal, behavioural and physical manifestations indicating that violence is imminent. Recognize it or not – and it is decidedly advantageous that you do – it is highly likely there will be some indicator prior to an attack. Non-verbal gestures should be prioritized; these are strong indicators of someone's intentions and true feelings. Gross motor movements often red flag someone who is adrenalized and about to explode.

If Necessary, Break Your Attacker's Body

To stop an assailant, Krav Maga primarily targets the body's vital soft tissue, chiefly the groin, neck, and eyes. To goal is to cause structural damage, not merely to hurt an aggressor. Other secondary targets include organs and bones such as the kidneys, solar plexus, knees, liver, joints, fingers, nerve centres, and other smaller fragile bones. The human body is affected by anatomical injury in a foreseeable manner; with training and a basic understanding of how the human body responds to trauma, you can generally predict how your counter-attacks will affect the attacker's subsequent movements or capacity to continue violence against you. For example, if you knee someone in the groin, you are likely to drop the attacker's height level thus exposing the base of the skull or the back of the neck to a vertical combative strike.

Israeli Krav Maga's Tactical Ten Commandants

1. Israeli Krav Maga works against any attacker; the key is your mind-set. Never accept defeat or surrender. If you can breathe, you can fight. Do what you must to prevail.

2. Assess your surroundings. Common sense, panning the environment along with basic precautions and a confident demeanour minimize your chances of being attacked.

3. Conflict avoidance or non-violent conflict resolution is always your best solution.

4. A few mastered core tactics go a long way and are highly effective.

5. Street violence has no rules (notwithstanding post-incident legal considerations if you were legally justified in your actions).

6. The essence of Krav Maga is to neutralize an attacker quickly by striking vital points and organs or applying choking or joint-breaking pressure.

7. A strategy to end your attacker's fighting ability is paramount while moving off the line of attack and using simultaneous defence and attack.

8. Footwork and body positioning allow you to simultaneously defend and attack allowing you to perform retzev or 'continuous combat motion.'

9. Optimally, a Kravist will move quickly to a superior and dominant position or the 'dead side' to finish the fight.

10. Simultaneous (or near simultaneous) defence combined with overwhelming, decisive retzev counter-attacks.

89

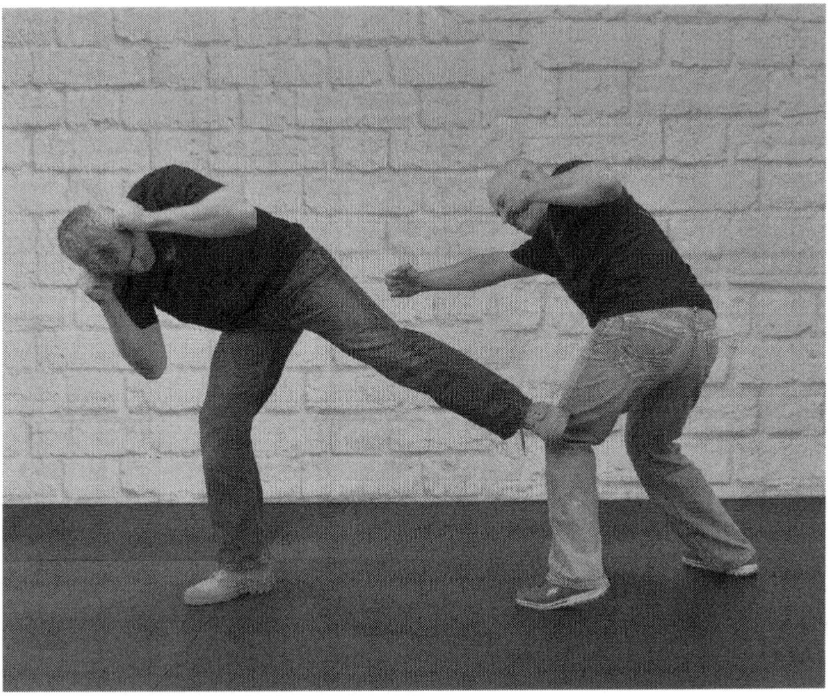

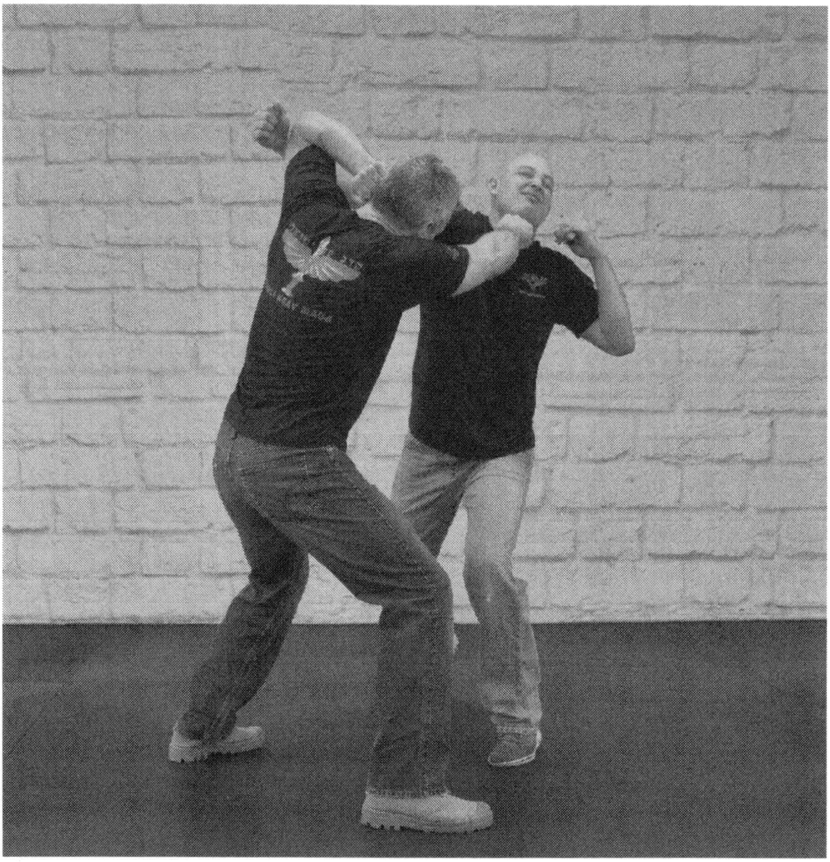

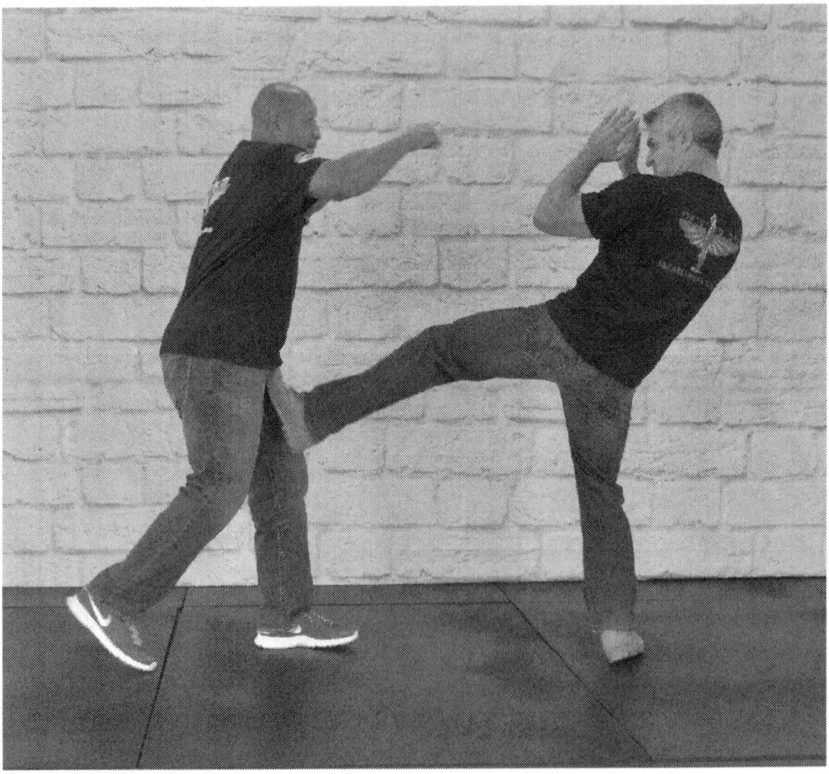

JEET KUNE DO - The Way of the Intercepting Fist
By Norm Willis

Bruce Lee started Wing Chun kung fu at the age thirteen in under Ip Man, developing it to include elements of fencing, which he learnt from his brother, and Tai Chi which he learnt from his father. Before moving to America in 1958, Bruce also won the Hong Kong boxing championships. Although he primarily moved to America to study philosophy at university, it was also partly due to the increasing number of fights Bruce was getting himself into back home.

Whilst in America, Bruce started to teach kung fu, and it is at this time that one of his students, Jesse Glover, introduced Bruce to grappling and judo.

The legend goes that after his fight in 1964 with Wong Jack Man, in which Bruce won but wasn't happy with his performance, he researched various arts in order to incorporate the best of their principals and training methods into one form, so in 1967 Jeet Kune Do was founded with its origins in Wing Chun, Western style boxing, fencing, wrestling, grappling, Ju-jitsu and judo.

Bruce Lee was way ahead of his time; whereas now Mixed Martial Arts is a household name, cross-training in different arts was unheard of at the time. Arguably therefore Jeet Kune Do is probably the original MMA, though unlike MMA - which it is predominantly used for sport - Jeet Kune Do (although it has elements of sport in it), is clearly a self-defence system used for street combat where the objectives are striking vulnerable targets on the body,

Jeet Kune Do has four ranges of combat: punching, kicking, trapping and grappling; where kicking is long-range, punching is mid-range, trapping and grappling are close-range. Each aim has a different purpose in disabling your opponent. For example, kicking range is designed to keep your attacker away from you whilst also trying to close the distance into the boxing range, and finally trapping and grappling; designed to trap or tie your opponent up in order to hit and not be hit yourself. The idea and principals of this fighting methodology still stand up today in real-life, street situations today; the idea of four ranges of combat: boxing, kickboxing, trapping and grappling all happen on the streets worldwide.

Bruce Lee's Jeet Kune Do has five ways of attack: Single Direct Attack (SDA), which could be classed as one punch or one kick; Attack By Combination (ABC), which could be a combination of punches, or a combination of punches and kicks; Hand Immobilisation Attack (HIA), which is also known as trapping, is the process where by you immobilise a limb in order to hit without being hit yourself. Attack By Drawing (ABD) can be done by leaving an exposed target to draw your attacker in and finally, Progressive Indirect Attack (PIA), very similar in its purpose to ABD, whereas the aim is to fake or feint an attack in order to move in a way so you can attack you opponent more effectively. These five ways of attack are also used in boxing and MMA.

The idea of the Centreline Theory originates from Wing Chun. The principals are to control your centre (your core) and attack your opponents' centre (their core); the one who controls the centre wins the attack. These are based on Jeet Kune Do's principles. Jeet Kune Do can be used for an attack based on one-on-one, or one against multiple opponents, empty hand or with weapons.

Are you going to run? Are you going to freeze? Or are you going to stand and fight? My own personal experience, after years of training in martial arts, tells me that a knowledge Jeet Kune Do will give you the tools to survive whatever the emotion or situation.

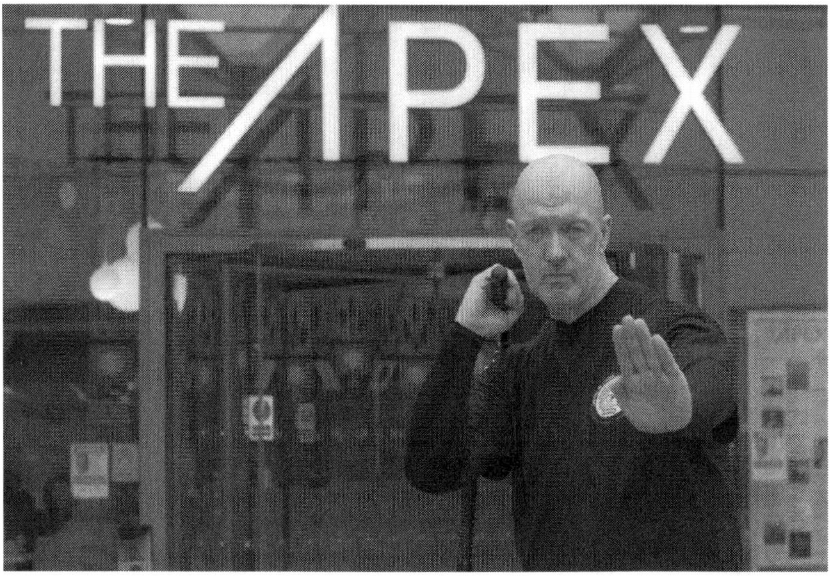
THE APEX

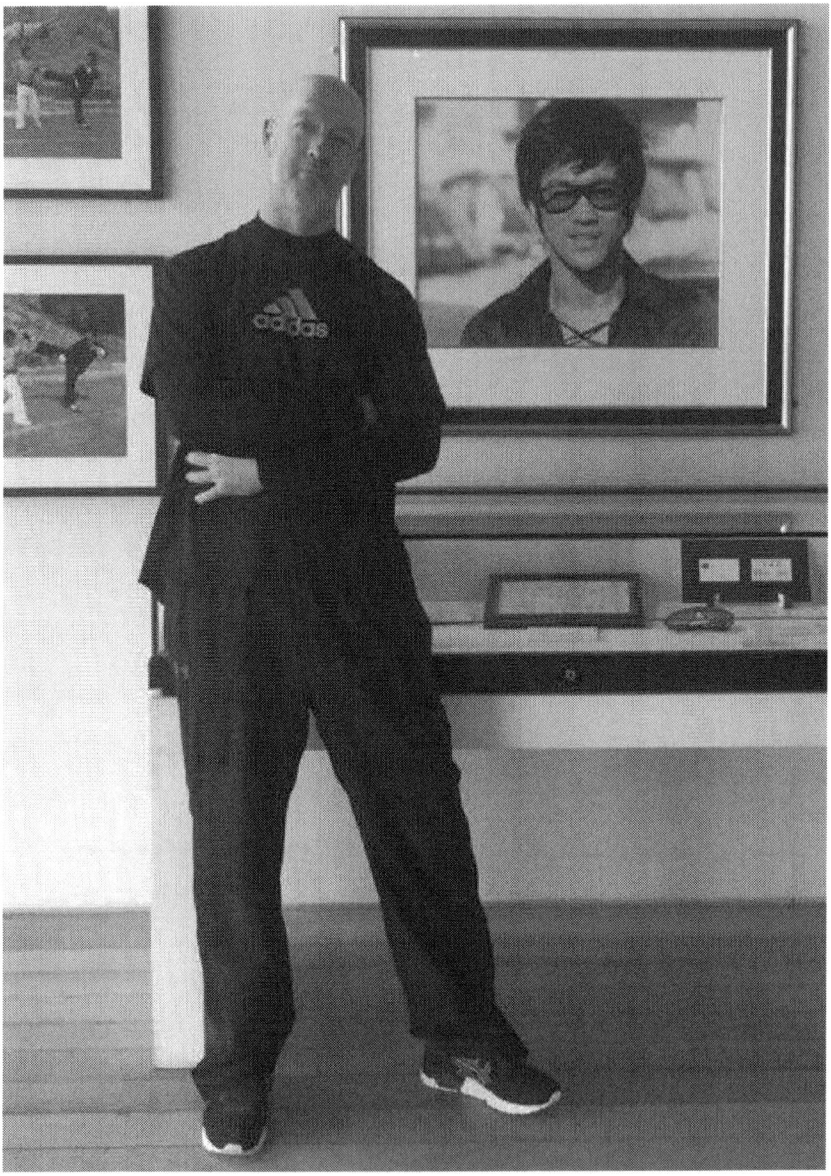

KARATE – As a Self-Defence System
By Tyrrel Francis

Karate developed on the Ryukyu Islands in what is now Okinawa, Japan. It was brought to the Japanese mainland in the early 20th Century, and then systematically taught across Japan after the Taishō era - a period in the history of Japan dating from July 30, 1912, to December 25, 1926, coinciding with the reign of the Emperor Taishō.

The art of karate receives a lot of negative reports as a self-defence system. It is almost as though it has somehow gone out of fashion since its introduction to the West, mainly by American service personnel who had practised the art while stationed on Okinawa after the Second World War. After World War II, Okinawa became an important United States military site, and karate became popular among servicemen; it wasn't long before karate schools began appearing across the world.

Karate in Japanese is from kara 'empty' and te 'hand'. Karate is now predominantly a striking art using punching, kicking, knee strikes, elbow strikes and open-hand techniques such as knife-hands, spear-hands, and palm-heel strikes.

The common claim that karate is less effective than other arts for self-defence comes mainly from misunderstanding the purpose of the training, especially during the initial stages. It takes many years to become proficient in the art of karate, and contrary to the belief of many non-practitioners, achieving a black belt is merely the beginning, and the training prior to that is just the groundwork. The purpose of moving up and down in lines, in deep stances, repetitively practising techniques, and the dedication to kata as a training method, is to build muscle memory, and lay the foundations for more advanced and dynamic training later on. Nobody would actually attempt to fight in this way in a live situation. As the practitioner becomes more advanced, shallower stances are introduced, as is the practice of more free-flowing and unscripted drills, within a disciplined and ritualised format. Sometimes, the practice of other arts gives a clue as to the purpose of the way karate is learned. The way karate punches are structured, encourages the use of the legs to generate power through the hips, using the same principles as throwing a punch in boxing. The longer, deeper stances become more transitional in free-flowing situations, even though the more advanced karateka will still practice 'basics' to maintain muscle memory and good form.

Looking at American Kenpo, a martial art evolved from the Chinese Kempo, gives us further clues as to some of the techniques practised in karate, especially some of those contained in kata forms. Karate is mainly thought of as a striking art, but the system also employs joint locks, throws and take-downs. These are not generally grappling techniques like those included in Ju-jitsu, but some of them resemble the standing defence of arts like Aikido. Many of what are initially practised as blocks, are revised at a more advanced stage as striking and breaking techniques, with the preparation being used as a parrying to set up the finishing blow or manoeuvre.

Karate is best learned from a young age in order to lay the necessary foundations, as it is a longer, more progressive journey to master than some other fighting styles and systems, but that does not make it any less effective, and it is never too late to begin learning either. However, a quick fix cannot be expected with karate, and this is perhaps one of the mistakes that people make with the art; impatiently wanting to become effective and proficient almost immediately. There is a gulf between being able to do something and doing it well - a person can learn the basic of a musical instrument within a short space of time, but to make music with it takes a lifetime of dedication. Part of the karate and combat sports ethos is making the training part of a way of life.

In conclusion, where karate is seen and accepted as a form of art, discipline and health and fitness training, for which it is an excellent practice, it cannot be discounted as an effective system of self-defence either. It has worked for centuries, applied in different ways, and forever having to adapt to the ever-evolving world. It is still practised worldwide by a variety of people of all ages and abilities, and has - and will continue to be - used as a form of self-defence with varying degrees of success, depending on the circumstances and the abilities of the practitioner.

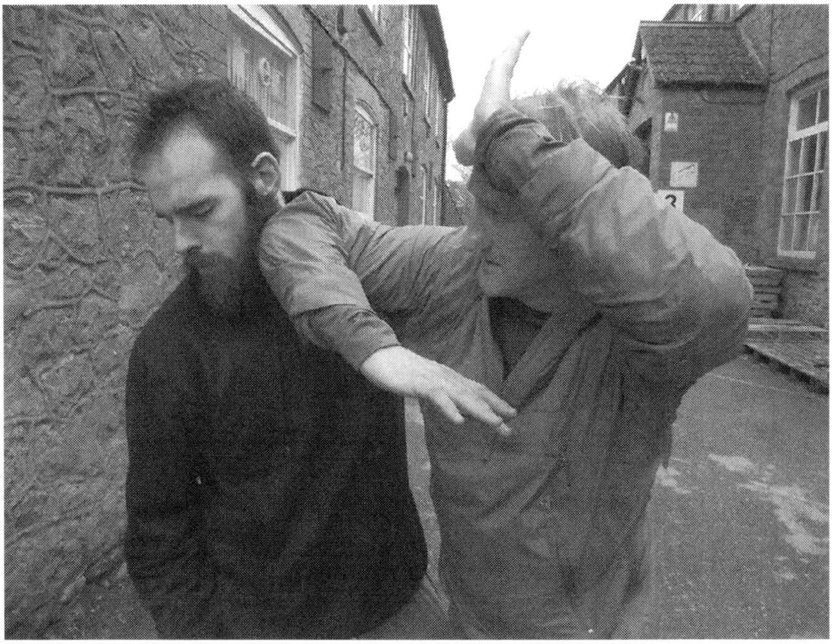

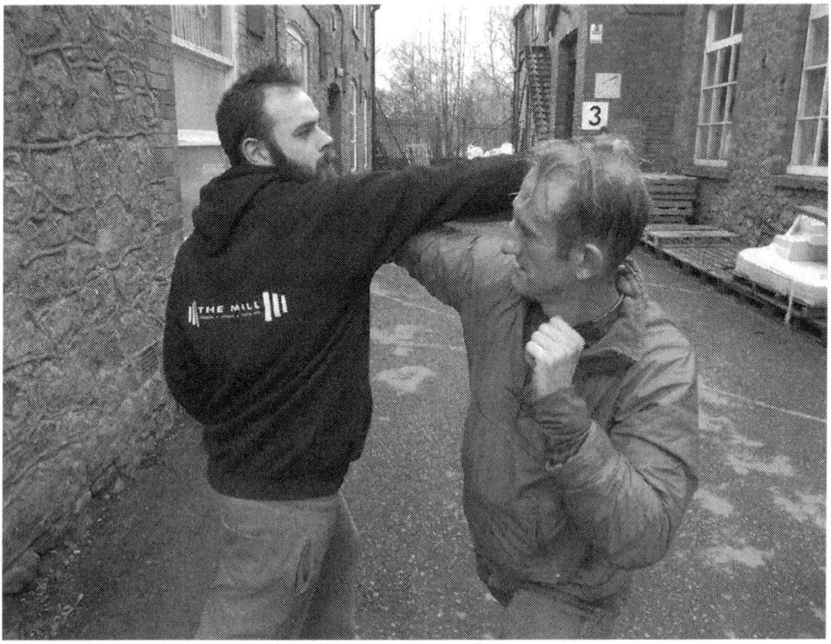
3
THE MILL

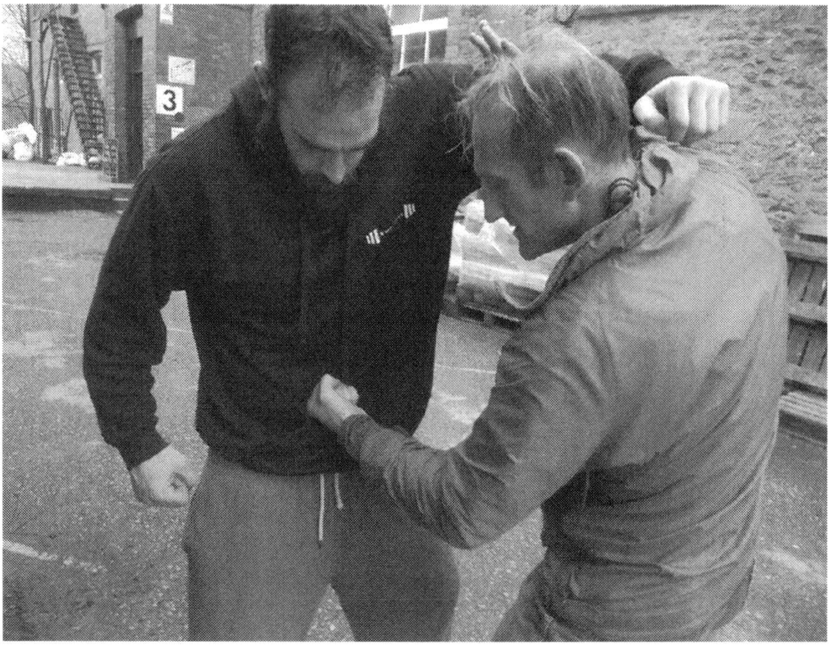
3

KNIVES & EDGED WEAPONS AWARENESS PROGRAMME (KEWAP) - Pragmatic, Time-Friendly and Highly Effective

By Steven Timperley

KEWAP was devised in 2009 by national and international award winning instructor Steven Timperley, who is also a former UK military specialist instructor (twenty-two years loyal service), and several years loyal service with the Nottinghamshire Special Police Constabulary. Impressively, to date there are now approximately four hundred fully qualified KEWAP instructors in towns and cities in England, and parts of Wales, delivering KEWAP to their respective communities. Also, there are KEWAP Instructors presently located in the Middle East delivering training to security personnel and law enforcement agencies. And Steven has also taught specialist KEWAP trainers from the British Transport Police (BTP) who now work of the KEWAP module when delivering training to front-line BTP officers.

In the main, KEWAP has been specifically designed to be highly educational and though provoking in regards to the factual content documented in the respective power-point presentations. It comes in two formats; the adult variant and the unique under 18s variant. Both formats cover many subjects including awareness, avoidance, everyday personal safety protocols, the law & knives, as well as physical response options instruction (over 16s). KEWAP physical response options are suitable for those who have little or no self-defence training or martial arts experience, which makes it pragmatic, time-friendly to instruct and highly effective (attack response options).

KEWAP can be delivered in a half day course format presentation which covers a wealth of information regarding the urban edged weapon threat and personal safety protocols. The full Knives & Edged Weapons Awareness Programme (6 hours) is the most comprehensive course of its kind available in the UK to date which includes defence against edged-weapons training. Pure defence against edged weapons training can be delivered for those who seek physical response options instruction only. Specialised training for military, police and security personnel is also undertaken upon request and therefore is bespoke to those respective sectors.

Over the past ten years there has been a massive push to educate young people in the UK not to carry knives. So, in order to reduce youth related knife crimes, it is now widely thought that educating those below the age of eighteen to the dangers and the implications of carrying knives is a must. And the fact still remains that many who attend education in both inner-city areas, and affluent towns, carry bladed articles and this problem is not going away. In the main, not all victims of a knife related crimes are members of urban street gangs. Sadly, the larger percentage of those under sixteen years-old who fall prey to knife related crimes, are in fact decent individuals going about their normal daily patterns of life. So, response options instruction is available to those over sixteen years-old. This is because those aged sixteen and over are more socially active. In turn, this training covers distancing, escape route selection, use of cover / barriers, deflection drills and other pragmatic response options.

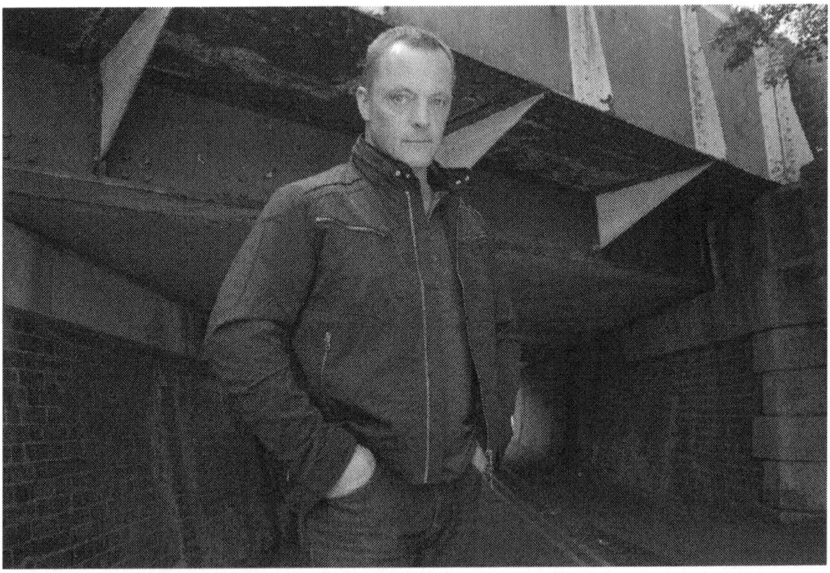

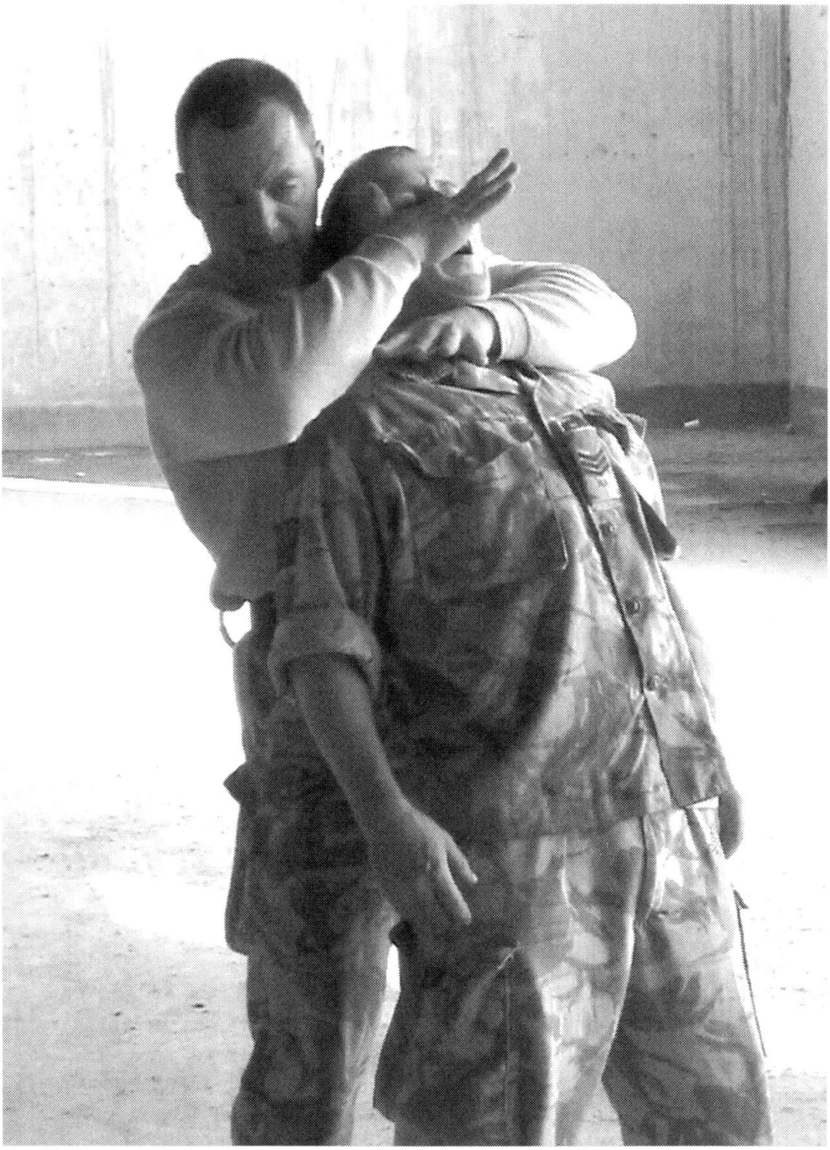

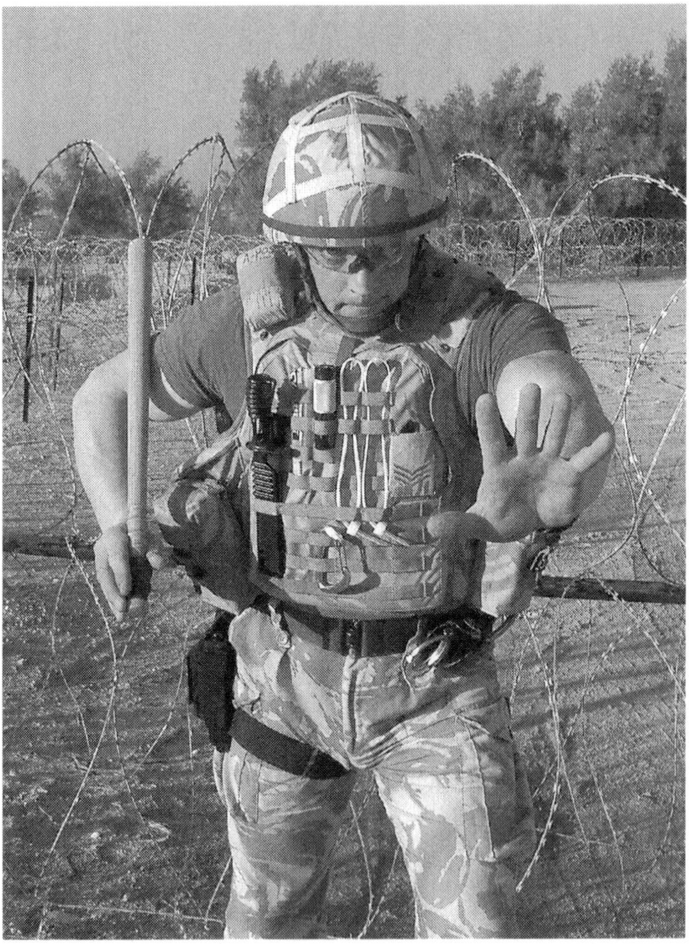

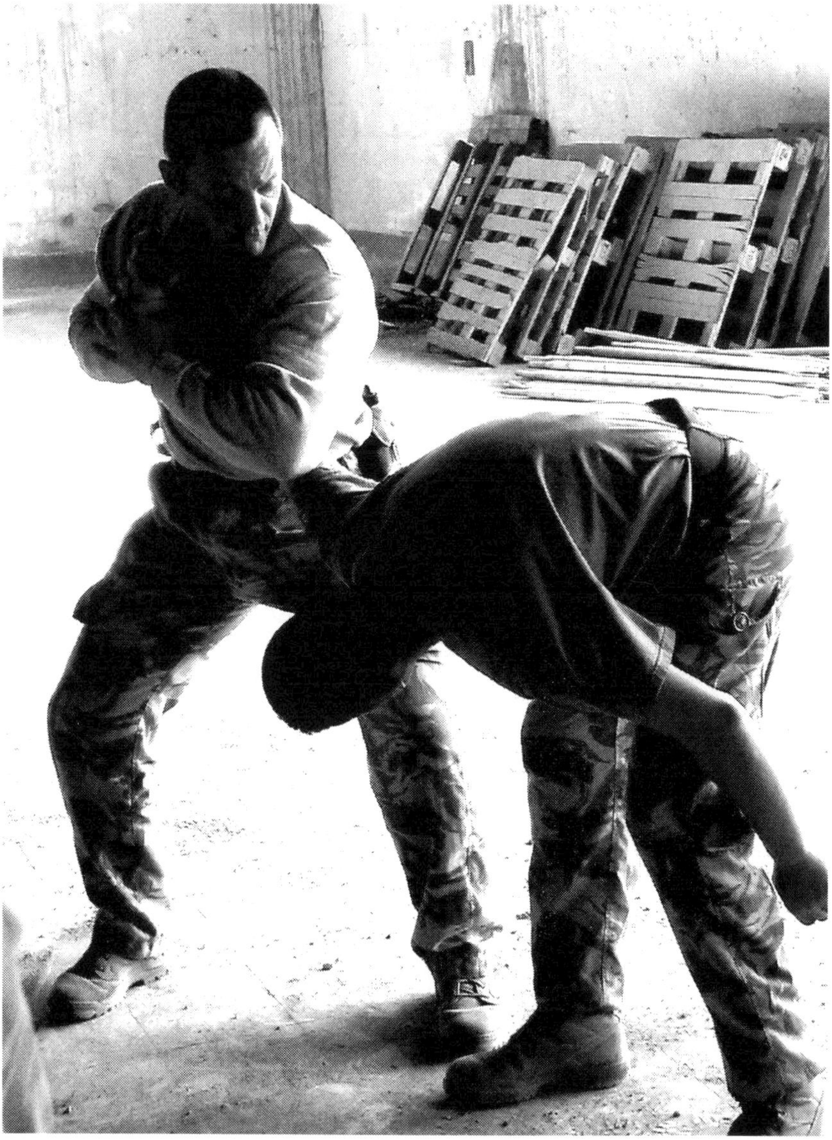

KWON BUP - A Study in How a Martial Art Dies... and is Resurrected

By Al Case

The Early Origins

Kwon Bup (Gwonbeop) is a Korean word meaning 'Fist Method.' Thus, when you hear the full title of an art with roots in Korea, such as 'Kang Duk Won Kwon Bup,' the meaning is 'House for Espousing Virtue Fist Method.' Kwon Bup qualifies as an ancient art, as it was practised during the Three Kingdoms period of Korean history; between 37 BC and 660 AD. During that time, each of the Three Kingdoms established institutions for training warriors. For about one thousand years, these institutions included mostly kicks and punches, and held hand-to-hand contests on public holidays, ending only with the Mongol invasion of Korea (1231 - 1392).

Some four hundred years after the Mongol invasion, in 1591, with no strong military to protect itself, Korea was conquered by Japan, which intended to use Korea to invade China. Eventually the Japanese armies were halted by the combined efforts of the Chinese and Koreans.

In September 1593, Korean Prime Minister Yu Song-Nyong attempted to resurrect the Korean army. This effort is referenced in *Jin Xiao Shin Shu (Manual of New Military Tactics)*, written by Qi Jiguang, and in this ancient manual we have our first official and verifiable reference to the art of Kwon Bup. In the manual, there is description of thirty-two methods of hand-to-hand combat. In 1598, the Korean government decided to adopt parts of the manual; the result was the *Muye Jebo (Compendium of Several Martial Arts)*, which included twelve additional fighting methods. Later, six more methods were added, bringing the total fighting methods to fifty. These last six seemed to have been designed for ground grappling. Eventually though, these methods fell out of favour as they seemed to have limited combat effectiveness, and even General Qi Jiguang ,the author of the *Muye Jebo* himself, held that they were of little use on the battlefield. Finally, with the appearance of rifles, revolvers and breech loading artillery, the training methods of Kwon Bup were exchanged for small unit tactics, and modern warfare did not include an in-depth study of hand to hand fighting methods.

In conclusion, it seems that although there was a viable martial art created by the Koreans, there were a number of weaknesses which included a tournament mentality develop by the early institutions, Confucian influences, and nationalism.

Various influences, and the lack of real records, the Korean martial arts were far from extinguished; after World War 1, and despite a lack of 'usefulness' on the battlefield, the martial art experienced a profound resurrection in Korea.

Modern Day Incarnations

One of the most influential of the Korean martial artists after World War 1 was a young fellow named Byung In-Yoon. As a child Yoon was obsessed by martial arts. Even though his hand was partially crippled (a fall into a fire), he wanted to study martial arts, and so he lurked at the windows of the local martial arts training hall, made himself useful, and was eventually accepted as a student by the local Master. Yoon envisioned nothing but a career in the martial arts, but initially it was not to be; he was called upon by his family to go away to highschool. However, this proved not to be the end of his martial arts career, but a new beginning. While at school he became acquainted with karate instructor Kanken Toyama, agreed to trade arts with Mr. Toyama, and eventually became the lead instructor in Mr. Toyama's school. Yoon would eventually go home and teach karate, and was instrumental in the establishment of the early 'Kwans' (houses), and his version of Korean karate would become well-known throughout Korea, and even be credited with influencing the art of Tae Kwon Do (the way of the hand and the foot). However, there was a sad ending; Yoon was eventually taken by his older brother to fight for North Korea during the Korean War. Because of his great skill, he was prevented from being repatriated to South Korea and, forced to go to North Korea, ended up working in a cement factory, returning home at an advanced age and in poor health.

One of the people Yoon taught karate to was a young man named Chul Hee Park. It was Park who would be instrumental in the establishment of the Kang Duk Won. He, in turn, would teach a young man named Norman Rha. Norman Rha would eventually travel to the San Francisco Bay area, and it would be there that the story of Kwon Bup would resurrect in powerful fashion.

A New Beginning

The martial arts gained ground slowly in the United States. During the '50s there were almost no schools of karate, and the few that were there, called themselves judo. One of the early martial arts schools was begun by a San Francisco police officer who had been injured in the line of duty; Officer Don Buck was hit on the head with a lead pipe and subsequently removed from duty. He would rehabilitate himself, becoming a physical cultist supreme, and opened a branch of Kyokushinkai karate. Mr. Buck's first black belt and first instructor at his school was a young man named Robert (Bob) Babich.

One day a young Korean walked into the school. It was Norman Rha, fresh off the boat, and ready to do some karate. Don Buck, having rebuilt himself into a brawny, muscular specimen, looked down at the young Korean; doubtless he was not impressed by the skinny youth who could barely speak English. Still, the martial arts were heavy in ritual politeness, so Mr. Buck invited Norman to fight. Norman took on all comers, showing a lithe liquidity that confounded the stocky, 'stand and block' Kyukoshinkai practitioners. Finally Mr. Buck himself stepped out to confront the skinny kid from Korea. From all accounts, Norman stood up to the larger American well, and earned a rare and profound respect. Unfortunately, Norman's methods did not blend well with Mr. Buck's; Kyokushinkai was all about standing and punching until the other fellow downs, or you did. Norman Rha was a slippery cat with greasy fur and ball-bearing feet. The solution to this unworkable synthesis was quite interesting; Mr. Buck turned to Bob Babich and told him to work with Norman.

For four years Bob and Norman were like room-mates. Bob taught Norman English, and Norman taught Bob Kang Duk Won. Bob would go on to become a 6th degree black belt in the Kang Duk Won, and open one of the first schools in the United States. The school was located in San Jose, California and it was at this school, during the late '60s and early '70s, that I trained.

This was the time of legends in the Golden Age of Martial Arts. People like Chuck Norris and Joe Lewis would fight in tournaments. Kenpo karate would franchise across the United States. Arts like Aikido and Tai Chi Chuan would begin their inroads. Martial arts were exploding, and right in the middle of the explosion, like the ignition point of an atomic bomb, Bruce Lee would make his appearance. Bob ignored it all. Although he had some of the highest quality black belts in the world at his school, he refused to open more schools. Instead he preferred to train, to perfect his art, and to teach those who really wished to learn the martial arts. The only change he made to the Kang Duk Won, was the introduction of several forms he devised himself. These forms were called Basics 1 - 2, Sets 1 - 3, the Kicking Form, and the Stick Set. Eventually Mr. Babich reached the highest level of art. He proved this by thrusting his single index finger through a piece of wood and leaving a hole. *How does one gain this ability? How does one do something that is superhuman? How does one go beyond what is accepted as human?* The answer is through training, through fanaticism and through doing what other people think they can't do.

And, in a rare case, people leave behind a written records of their martial arts journeys, but Bob left no written record, thus,over the years I wrote down the bulk of forms, and their techniques, and eventually published it to record, and thus remember, the genius of the man.

And we come to the questions: Is this true Kwon Bup? Does this bear resemblance to the original Korean fighting methods? Koreans had their own martial arts and held on to their fighting methods. Koreans withstood invasion and battle to hold onto their culture and identity. Koreans built the Kang Duk Won and they exported it. It was a Korean (Mas Oyama) who trained Don Buck and who trained Mr. Babich. So therefore is Kwon Bup, as originated by Mr. Babich, a true Korean art?

I propose that all the connections are good; not because of lineage, or acquaintance, but because of those who passed the martial arts down to others are inspired, they are obsessed, they are fanatic. The heart of karate - of all martial arts - is a spirit, a spirit that is immune to nation, religion, tournament, even vested interest. That spirit is what drives a man to thrust his finger through a board and leave a hole. It is that spirit that inspired the Kwon Bup of thousands of years ago, and it is that spirit that resided in the heart of Bob Babich.

Conclusion A final Word

One day in the middle of the 1970s two Koreans walked into the San Jose Kang Duk Won. They offered advanced ranking to Bob and all his black belts if they would come over to this new art called Tae Kwon Do. Bob refused. Yet this was not the end of it. Bob belonged to the Korean Martial Arts Association and possibly because of this 'conflict' with Taekwondo, Bob left the organization, and therefore he was no longer able to present the label of Kang Duk Won for his art. And so Bob decided to start his own organization, and he renamed his art. He renamed it Kwon Bup. I was at Bob's house one day and happened to notice a book on Bob's coffee table. It was a big, thick thing, filled with pictures and written in the Korean language. I asked Bob (pictured below) *"I didn't know you could read Korean?"* Bob: *"I can't."* I asked: *"How do you read it?"* Bob: *"I don't, I just look at the pictures."* I asked: *"Do you know the name of the book?"* Bob: *"Kwon Bup."*

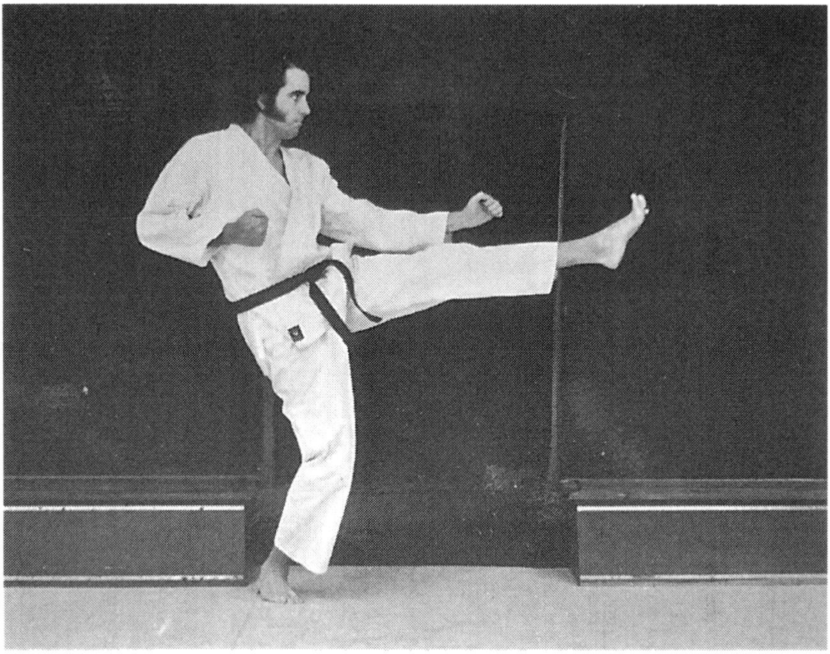

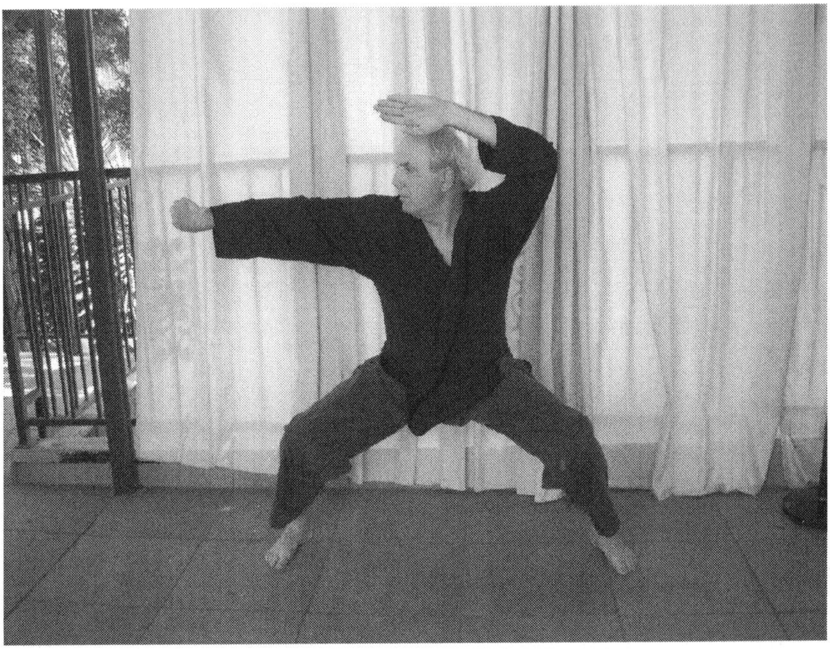

MEANSTREETS SELF-DEFENCE SYSTEM - Raw, Brutal and it Works
By Russell Jarmesty

At the age of seventeen Russ started studying traditional style karate, attaining black belt status after just three years This ignited his passion for martial arts; he was keen to explore other disciplines and to further his understanding of the arts, so he sought other clubs and influences to better his knowledge. While still attending karate sessions, Russ also began learning from Hanshi Trevor Roberts, which unfortunately caused some political friction between him and his karate instructor, and so Russ left the club and moved across to continue his studies under Trevor. Trevor is two-time British Olympic Freestyle Wrestling Champion; four-times British Ju-jitsu champion; British Sambo champion; Grand Master; 8th dan Ju-jitsu; 6th dan Shiai-Jitsu; 6th dan Combat Sambo; and Russian Master of Sport. Trevor has trained over thirty British Champions and has been a doorman for over thirty years.

Russ instantly fell in love with the brutality and honesty of his art and his way of teaching; Russ had found his new home. While training under Trevor, one of Russ' oldest friends was attacked and badly injured. This stirred up a gut-felt desire in Russ to do something about stopping this sort of brutal and unnecessary attack from ever happening again. After a chat with Trevor, Russ chose to begin working on the doors too. His reasons were two-fold: Firstly, to catch as many bullies as he possibly could, and secondly to see what martial arts and combat training actually worked in a real-deal fight.

Russ had his suspicions that the karate wouldn't work on the streets; to him karate just didn't look or feel like real fighting, However, he couldn't say the same for Trevor's Ju-jitsu, and he knew it was time to 'don the blacks' and see what it was all about.

Right from the start, Russ realised that he would have to bin 90% of the karate he had learned; although it had massively built up his speed and conditioning, and his knuckles were like steel, it was a little less than useless on the streets; the scenarios he was facing on the doors didn't include bowing and a respectful tap around; they involved deadly intent and people who wanted nothing more than to hurt you and leave you in a pool of your own blood. Ju-jitsu, on the other hand, fitted like a glove, and it was as if the scraps on the doors were just another training session. But there was still something missing; the art fit beautifully to his new lifestyle, but his fear and the nerves before a physical confrontation, never changed. And so the next stage was understanding and taking ownership of that good old thing called adrenaline; it was the missing link.

The feeling, the emotions, the control. Control is key in a street fight.

Adrenaline, fear or liquid gold - whatever name you want to give it - offers qualities that are universal and can't be changed. If you mistake this adrenaline for fear, it will freeze you to the spot, fill you with self-doubt and make you feel scared... and you don't want to fight someone else when you're already fighting yourself. So this is the key; harnessing that adrenaline and focusing its effect on you and learning how to channel it. It's your very own super-power; it's liquid gold. It anaesthetizes you to pain and makes you faster and stronger than you've ever been. Popeye had spinach, we have adrenaline. You've heard stories of people lifting up cars due to extreme situations. How? Simple, they used the adrenaline and didn't let it use them - don't fear it and don't make it your friend. Understand it, take ownership of it and use it. Once you've spent time feeling it, controlling it and finally taking ownership of it, you're 90% there. Unfortunately, you can't start to understand adrenaline if you've never stepped into the fire; and this is the biggest part of Russ's training now.

Russ continued to learn and grow under the guided hand of Trevor Roberts but when Russ broke his neck it put a stop to his training and door work for some time. Despite this, Russ continued to attend classes, watching and absorbing all Trevor had to offer even though he could not take part. Watching and listening still gave him an opportunity to learn and develop his expanding knowledge from a new perspective.

Once recovered, Russ went looking for a club, any club, that would complement his style. Although karate was his original style, Russ felt that Ju-jitsu offered more of what he needed to influence the development of his application; it was more geared towards up-close techniques that suited to his combat style. This is when Russ ventured into Russian Sambo and, from that point on, he stayed in-house with his own students, friends and door lads, and spent the following years piecing together all the gold from each style to make it applicable for the world he was in - the 'Door' world.

Another of Russ' main influences at that time was Geoff Thompson, renowned in the self-defence world. Geoff is a writer, a teacher and self-defence instructor holding 8th degree black belt in karate, 1st degree black belt in judo, and 1st degree black belt in Aikido. He has also written several books on self-defence, martial arts and fear control. Russ read everything Geoff wrote - including his first book called *Watch My Back* - watched his videos and implemented his teachings into his own training. Alongside Trevor Robert and Geoff Thompson, Russ drew much of his knowledge and experience from old-school doormen; many of them may have been lacking in techniques but their mindset and experience more than made up for it. He watched every move they'd make; how they talked, how they stood, when they'd fight and when they wouldn't. Russ knew that experience is key, and the more he learnt the more he realised that his karate training was going to get used less and less.

Door work really influenced the way that Russ learnt, taught and developed his style of combat. Whenever there was an incident during his time at work, he would analyse how it had played out and rework the methods of control and manipulation used to subdue or remove an individual. Russ would then take that incident and apply it to his classes, tweaking and moulding and shaping the encounter to understand how his approach could be improved. Russ would then wait for that incident to come again so he could test how he had trained to combat it.

Survival was Russ' main motivator; knowing that each time an altercation took place the ambulance would get called, Russ knew it was his job to ensure that the person taking the ride in it was going to be the trouble-maker, and not him. There was a period of time where Russ started to wonder if he was any better than person facing him; violence was the common ground between him and many of the people he would come up against. The difference was that he knew he was using violence to help innocent people; the public, the clubbers, the nicer side of society, while the trouble-makers were using their violence to dominate, control, manipulate and abuse. Like Russ always says; *the best defence against evil men is good people skilled in violence.*

Violence, once it's on the cards, is best dealt with instantly. Learn to punch hard, know dirty places to go, learn how to dig deep and give yourself an extra dose of adrenaline. It's easy once you can control it. Russ' art comprises of power, speed and things that hurt.

In the outside world, don't over complicate things and don't over complicate philosophies when it comes to fighting either. One simple thing that Russ believes is that, if you don't put pressure on them, then they will put pressure on you. If you know it's going to kick-off, you'd be stupid to let them get in first. You can talk to some people, even plead, but there's always a minority that just need a crack before they can listen. Pain is a great motivator for people to stop fighting. If it hurts... it works.

Politeness is a huge key too; Russ made a very big point of being as nice and polite as possible whilst being a hair-trigger away from being the exact opposite. If you growl and snarl before you hit someone, then they always see it coming; if you smile and offer polite words, it's easier to get the shot in. The savvier you become in verbal sparring, the less likely you are to get your hands dirty. This leans to the principle of what Russ teaches; *nobody wants to fight but if you are in a fight, then you have to fight.* If all options of discussion are exhausted and you find yourself in a fight, you will definitely be fighting. Learning to become comfortable with being uncomfortable is the key. Russ' own insecurities meant that when he would see someone in front of him as massive threat, he would destroy that threat quickly. As Russ grew and understood more through his training and work life, he began to see each threat as more of a challenge. This in itself meant that Russ' approach and view of altercations altered again; learning not to over react just because he got hit with a few harsh words and harsh stares. Knowing that when the violence does start and kind words and polite gestures won't stop it, so it is only with violence that Russ can makes sure that all his students understand and live on the very basic principles.

Russ has been surrounded by like-minded people, not just martial artists, but doormen, friends and experienced individuals all willing to offer what they know to help strengthen and empower others to be able to protect themselves efficiently and effectively. Russ' instructors were everyone he was stood around, regardless of their age or style. One of these individuals was Jimmy Kelly, Jimmy, known as 'The Shark', is a Kempo, Ju-jitsu and Krav Maga practitioner. Jimmy holds level 1 and 2 ABA boxing licence - with over a hundred fights, and near forty years experience - a level 1 in British freestyle wrestling, fourteen years of training in catch wrestling, a 4th dan in Kempo, a 2nd dan in applied Ju-jistu under Hanshi Trevor Roberts, and an Esrima instructor with Warriors Escrima. Jimmy is qualified as an instructor in Urban Krav Maga under Stewart Mcgill and a KAPAP instructor; a full instructor with the BCA. Jimmy is brown belt under the SDF, and a master in combat under the SDF. He worked as a door supervisor all over Manchester and bodyguard for over twenty-three years.

Russ and Jimmy still train together now, Jimmy teaches at Russ' club and holds seminars together with Russ and other martial arts professional. Russ knows that these relationships are like no other; something that binds people together, stronger than ever when fighting side-by-side.

MeanStreets Self Defence System was formed from what Russ took from each style; from karate the speed, power and timing, as well as his golden front kick that has saved him more times that he can count. From JU-Jitsu Russ took the pain of every lock, choke, face bar, joint manipulation and anything that snaps. As well as this, Russ enjoyed the mauling side but getting in close with all these techniques is useless without the golden ingredient; mind-set. Russ had the luxury of already knowing what he wanted to achieve, and he knew that without the correct mindset, even the best punch in the world, if it was delivered with nervousness and fear, would have little effect on ten-year-old girl let alone 6ft2, 20st monster who wants to put you away quick. Russ keeps it simple; if people wanted a fight then he will gladly show them what a real fight looks like.

Working on the doors and testing MeanStreets in real-life scenarios completed the system and, for the last ten years, this is all Russ has taught; it's raw, brutal and it works. Russ now travels up and down the country holding MeanStreets seminars, runs a full-time academy in Atherton with over two-hundred students and has ten instructors, with backgrounds ranging from doormen, army veteran's, long-serving policemen and well established martial artists, teaching MeanStreets banner across the country. All his instructors are highly experienced in the world of violence, and Russ knows the importance of experience when teaching real self-defence and passes on to his instructors everything he has experienced.

If you can avoid violence, please, please do. But if you can't, then make sure you get in first and get in hard. Most importantly, keep your wits about you and if talking doesn't work just do what you have to do, quickly, and get out of there.

MeanStreets is a functioning martial art that can save your life.

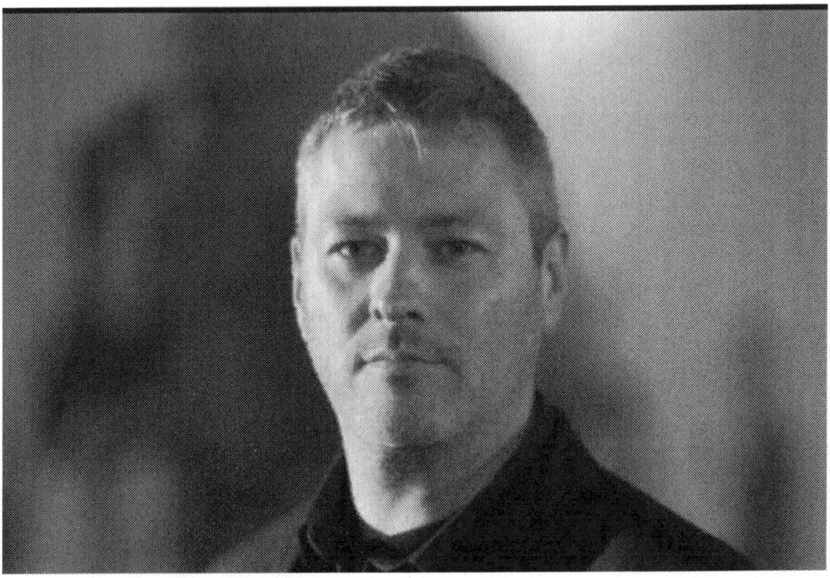

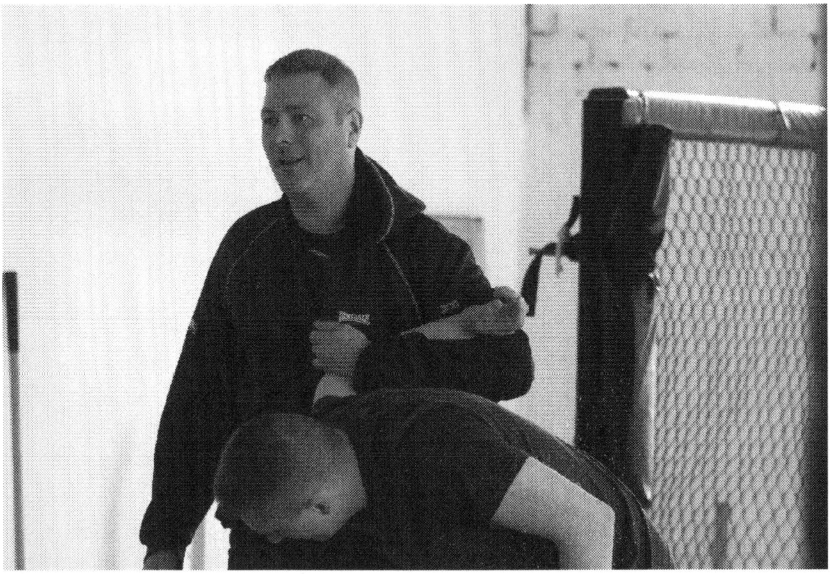

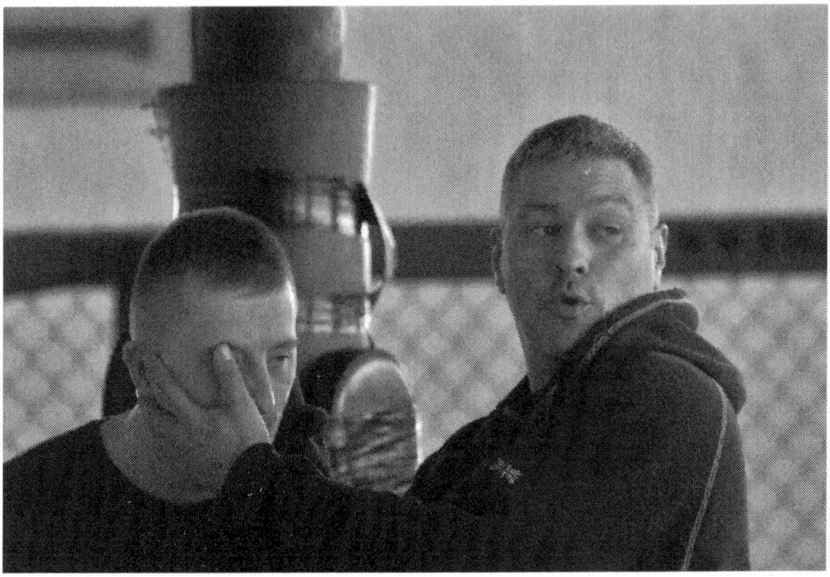

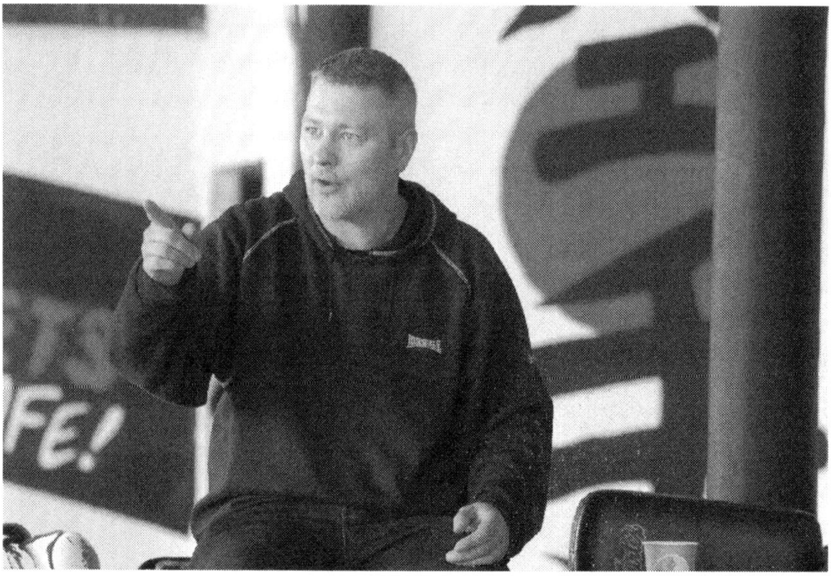

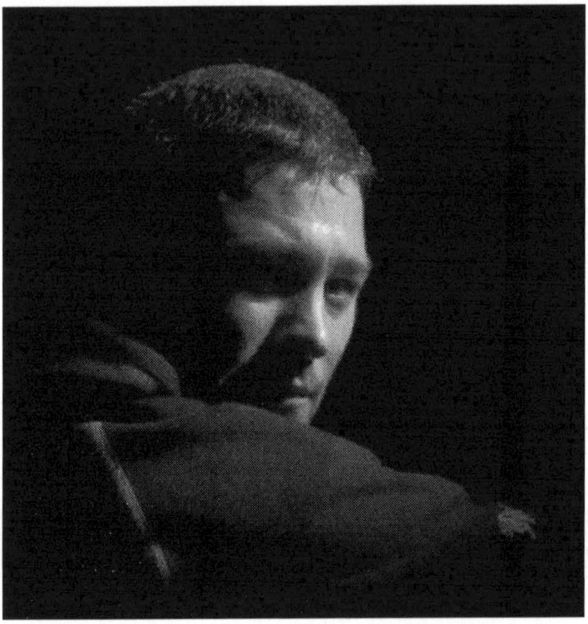

MUAY THAI – As a Self-Defence System
By Tyrrel Francis

When somebody mentions Muay Thai - or what some people refer to as Thai boxing - I'm willing to bet the first images that spring to mind are not necessarily as a self-defence system but more likely of two Thais in a boxing ring with extended guards, brutalising each other's legs by striking them with their shins.

It is true that Muay Thai is a combat sport, as is Western boxing, kickboxing and MMA, but it is also a system steeped in history and tradition. In the same way that judo has its roots in Ju-jitsu, one of the ancient arts used by the Samurai, Muay Thai was born out of Muay Boran, the ancient fighting system used by the Thai warriors of old. Unlike judo, which was created initially as a form of physical training for children before it became a popular combat sport, Muay Thai was immediately established as a sporting spectacle, when warriors in peace time needed a source of income, and would fight each other to entertain crowds, who would pay to watch, and bet on the outcome.

However, there is much opposition for promoting a combat sport as a system of self-defence, as it can be argued that fighting in a ring or cage, to a set of rules, under the observation and control of a referee is nothing like a street self-defence situation, and that it is likely that an attacker with either a different skill-set, or without any formal fight training will fight very differently. Both of these are valid points. The objective when being attacked, or defending others, is different to that in a competitive arena, where the aim is to defeat an opponent who has trained for the encounter. There are no surprises when two competitors step into the ring or cage to test their skills against each other. It reaches a conclusion, whether somebody is knocked-out or stopped in some way, or the judges make a decision after the time has elapsed. A self-defence situation is much more spontaneous, and the protagonist may strike without warning. Their objective will be different to that of the target, who will have one goal; to get away without being injured. These encounters tend not to last as long as a competitive bout, and the participants may not be trained athletes, and are often under the influence of alcohol or other intoxicating substance.

However, it is also very difficult to recreate this situation with a purposely designed self-defence system or traditional martial arts. What combat sports have in common with self-defence situations is that they are both high-pressure, fluid and intense experiences. Combat sports force the practitioner to work under pressure, with the pulse racing and no script. Surviving an ugly street situation, such as an unprovoked attack in a bar, requires heart, courage and bloody-mindedness; all qualities needed in a combat sports competitor, and Muay Thai is no exception to this.

Muay Thai employs long-to-close range techniques, from spectacular kicks to the head and body, to working from a close-range clinch, which is the link between striking and grappling with an opponent or an attacker. The ability to move constructively when in close quarters with an attacker can be invaluable, especially in a confined space such as a licensed premises. Clinch work is very tiring, especially to a person who has not practised it regularly. Mastering clinch work can not only stand a practitioner in good stead for winning a bout, but it can also give a means of wearing down an attacker and setting them up for a finishing technique, as well as giving a chance to assess any other threats, such as more than one attacker, move with a tactical purpose, and disengage constructively.

Translated as the *Art of Eight Limbs*, Muay Thai includes use of the body's harder weapons; the knees, shins and elbows, as well as the fists. To the uninitiated, receiving a well executed kick to the leg or body with the shin bone or the knee can be a powerful deterrent, and can slow a person down or limit their ability to give chase if their target makes a run for it. When landed to the head, knee or elbow strike, or a shin if the available space allows, is a potential knockout shot. There are many bones in the fists or feet, all vulnerable to breaking when hammered against a skull, which is designed to protect the brain and is therefore thick and solid. Landing these strikes in a fluid, unscripted situation however, can be very difficult, and having practised doing so in either sparring, or a competitive bout, can be invaluable. If you use the example of sword fighting; there may only be so many techniques that can be performed with a sword, but the best sword exponents were not the best because they knew more, but because they were well drilled and practised, and this can be applied to empty-handed fighting systems. The danger levels in street attack situations increases against an armed attacker, or against multiple attackers, but Muay Thai training develops awareness and reaction to danger as much as other arts. It is a very direct and explosive fighting system, and combines well with other arts such as Western boxing, wing chun or Ju-jitsu, and the training itself promotes health and body conditioning, which can be the difference between surviving and getting hurt. Compared to some other styles, there is nothing fancy about Muay Thai and, when taught properly, it is a very technical style used in a simplistic way, making the techniques more natural and relatively easy to program into the muscle memory, which makes self-defence more instinctive when under pressure. There are no rights and wrongs when it comes to self-defence, only survival, and Muay Thai is one of the styles that can be an effective tool, if applied correctly, in defending oneself - or another - from harm.

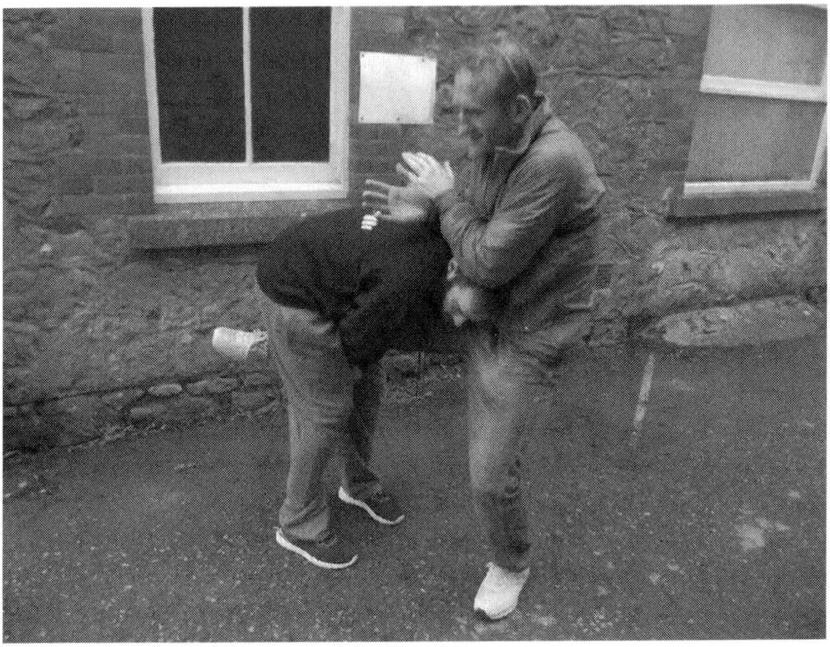

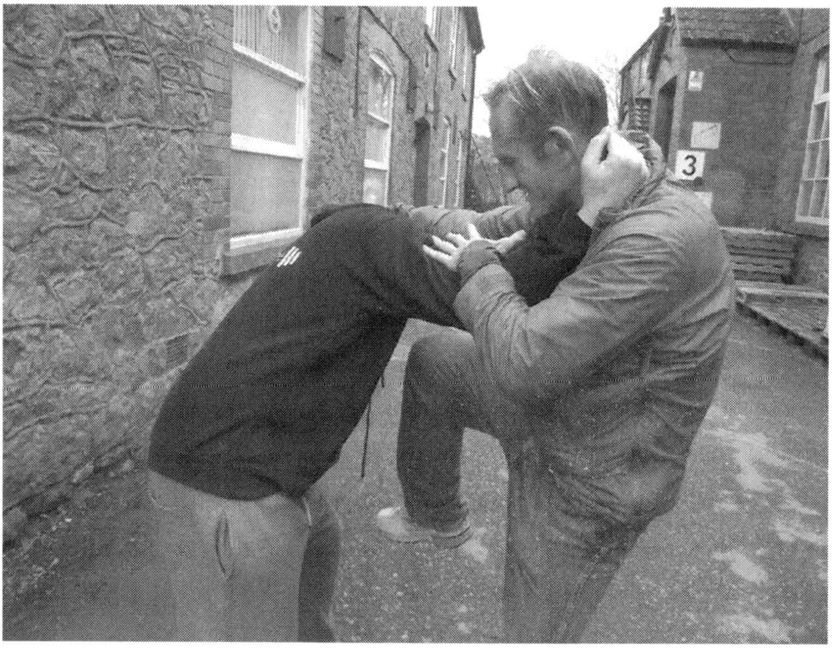
3

PANKRATION - The Grandfather of all Martial Arts
By Aris Makris

Like many others, I got into martial arts when I was nine years old, with the influence of Bruce Lee. It started with wanting to move the way he did; for me, his flair and fluidity was captivating, as well as his speed and dynamic movement. What started out as a young boy's dream to be like his idol soon turned into a necessity out of the need for survival. I lived in an area of Montreal that was a haven for gangs and poverty. The firstborn to hard-working Greek immigrant parents, the streets of Park Extension were as every bit dangerous as New York's Harlem or the Bronx. Back then, martial arts was not so much a luxury as a necessity and, given the craze of the 1970s era martial arts explosion, everyone and anyone was involved somehow in some form of martial arts.

As the son of Greek immigrants, Greek school was mandatory and while the word *Pagratio* - better known internationally in the English language as Pankration - was occasionally present in our elementary textbooks, I had no clue what it really was, or where I would wind up with it. I was completely fascinated with the martial arts and I couldn't get enough of them; I started in the typical Japanese arts and, as everyone else did, made my way around the various martial arts schools; being in the karate school only made me curious as to what was in the kung fu schools, and therefore felt I was missing out on what could be more knowledge gained. I was completely smitten and thirsty for any martial arts knowledge I could get my hands on. But that wasn't the prime mover and influence that led me to where I am today; Survival was the main driver.

I lived in a gang-torn area in which going to school in the morning and making it back home in the evening without a fight was rare. Then, at night time, we would form little gangs and meet up with other rival gangs and duke it out. Going through the traditional martial arts schools, I quickly realize that most did not actually teach me how to cope with what I encountered in the streets. I was thirteen or fourteen years-old and remember being completely confused with what was happening in real-life as opposed to what was going on in the dojos.

Having friends in other forms of sports like boxing, kick-boxing and judo prompted me to visit their gyms and that's where I found the beginning of my conflicts, and so, while my kicking was being developed by the traditional oriental arts, I soon began boxing and studying as judo as well, which taught me how to use my fists properly and fight on the ground. But my confusion to make sense of what the fight was all about was only beginning to grow.

I learned more about Pankration through one of my karate instructors, who introduced me to Mas Oyama's (a karate master who founded Kyokushin karate, considered to be the first and most influential style of full contact karate) book that stated; had it not been for the Greeks and Pankration, there would be no martial arts today.

That was the spark that set ablaze the rest of my life and never would I have thought that I would eventually become a world authority on Pankration and a Hall of Fame inductee.

With the rise of MMA, Pankration, has been - and continues to be - the topic of many conversations within the martial arts circles, and yet it is misunderstood by many modern fighters and coaches. In Greek, Pankration means *all encompassing and total powers*, which means you were allowed to strike with the fists, palms, elbows, knees, and included all forms of kicking techniques including front kicks, side kicks, round kicks and back kicks, as well as all forms of grappling and wrestling, and there were only two rules implemented in the ancient Olympic games for the sport of Pankration; no eye-gouging or biting - which included fish-hooking. Everything else was for the taking! This meant that one had to be adept in defending against all forms of strikes, including all forms of grappling and submissions. Small joint locks and breaks were allowed too, as well as head-shots to the temple and to the throat, including the cervical spine and the joints.

There are still huge differences between modern MMA and Pankration given today's mixed martial arts explosion in which fighters are becoming more complete in all areas of combat. While today in Mixed Martial Arts, many fighters will go to different disciplines and coaches to try to become more complete fighters, but in ancient times those studying Pankration would not have different coaches for the different areas of the style or art; for example a wrestling coach to teach wrestling skills, or a boxing coach to teach boxing skills. Boxers and wrestlers did not do anything other than box and wrestle, as so they were completely unfamiliar with the environment and dynamics of the Pankration tournament. Today this is a concept that most still can't seem to grasp. In Pankration one coach, called a Paidotrivis, taught it all and Pankratiasts were known to enter wrestling and boxing tournaments and come out victorious, while boxers and wrestlers never entered a Pankration tournament, simply because they were not equipped to handle all the various weaponry, techniques and tactics that Pankratiasts had trained in.

Pankratiasts we're also known to train alone and in seclusion of other fighters, and were considered the heavy armoury of the Olympic Games.

To quote the great Theban general Epaminondas (a Theban general and statesman of the 4th Century BC who transformed the Ancient Greek city-state of Thebes, leading it out of Spartan subjugation into a pre-eminent position in Greek politics); *"Economy of movement brings on efficiency of attack."*

Pankration is termed as the grandfather of all martial arts and chronologically it was the first ever documented complete fighting art. Originally it was thought that Pankration developed due to Alexander the Great, who pushed through the Indian Kush and introduced Pankration into Asia but, according to the ancient Greek texts, Pankration had found its way into the orient through trade routes many years before Alexander.

Having had the fortune of my childhood experiences on the streets, and having worked as a bouncer in clubs most of my adult life, gave me a better understanding of what I was missing in all the martial arts that I had studied. I realized that fighting was not one-dimensional, and that things happened on-the-fly and which were often out of your control. I realized that being able to mesh the stand-up and conquer the ground fighting was paramount if you were to survive in a real fight.

I learned early on that one cannot just combine techniques from different arts because it would be the same as trying to combine different engine parts of different cars to make one engine.

Armak Pankration is about principal, human behaviour and kinesiology. While Pankration today is also used as a sport, and is primarily founded in reality based training. Being able to combine the use of one's striking abilities in harmony with closing the gap in attaining an advantageous position over an opponent. Efficient striking and movement, as well as efficient striking and positioning on the ground in order to attain the goal to win over an opponent, either by a submission or a knockout.

I have had the opportunity to train many military units around the world such as the Italian and Portuguese Special Forces, as well as the American Special Forces, including units of the American DEA. I also been featured in a few documentaries portraying what modern Pankration is about.

At the Spartan Pankration Academy that houses Armak Pankration, we haven't reinvented the wheel but have tried to give it back its perspective, and to come close to that of what our ancient Spartan forefathers would have been doing had continued throughout the centuries.

PROGRESSIVE KENPO - An Advanced Form of Traditional Kempo

By Jonathan Hodgson

I started training in Kenpo, a more progressive form of the traditional Kempo, at the age of six, in Chard, Somerset. It's fair to say martial arts was, and has ever since been my biggest passion. My parents and several close relatives were teachers and professional sports coaches, so naturally my childhood was steeped in education. Living in a rural part of Somerset, I had a very active, outdoors life, including sports such as cricket, archery and gymnastics, alongside Kenpo. From my early teens I coached sports and lived and breathed martial arts and combat science, which all provided a great basis for what I do now.

I have always had a passion for weapons training and, despite the rule that only adults could learn weapons in Kenpo, I started practising with swords, sai, knives, sticks etc., from the age of twelve... asking instructors and older students to share their knowledge, reading every book and text I could get hold of, and inventing my own forms and techniques, utilising Kenpo as a starting point. To this day, people describe me as a maverick, and I think I always have been in that respect.

When I joined the senior Kenpo class aged fourteen, I started learning the Kenpo 'self-defence' techniques. This became my grounding for everything I do now. It's fair to say the Chard Kenpo Club had a reputation for being one of the 'harder' clubs to train at in the area. In fact, other clubs locally nicknamed us the Chard 'animals,' as we did improvise a lot and hit quite hard and with little protection. Therefore bruises and superficial injuries were absolutely constant. The upside of these years was the conditioning; though at a cost of occasional fractures and breaks, and an odd mixture of respect and contempt from other Kenpo clubs.

At the age of nineteen, I achieved my 1st degree black belt alongside Matt 'The Mill' Follain, and worked a lot with Neil Hazell, my instructor at the time. Neil Hazell is a great practitioner of Kenpo, though lesser known in the wider martial arts world. Around this time I realised that the fixed, rigid approach to training for real-world self defence was not practical for me, so I decided to break from the traditional structure and politics, and go with my instincts. I had already dabbled in other systems over the years, but knew that in educational terms, the right instructor will get you where you wish to be, almost regardless of their style. About this time I met two Ju-jutsu and Kobudo Sensei; Danny Clarke, and his Instructor Brian Carpenter. They were both ex-military, and for me this was a good sign for what I wanted to achieve. So I studied this for a few years, still training and teaching Kenpo while filling the gaps with anything useful and appropriate for progression and practicality. I attended many seminars, bought every useful book and hundreds of DVDs on anything potentially beneficial, and just studied it fanatically to absorb as much as possible, trying it in the dojo, and pressure-testing it.

The biggest influence on my work came from a chance meeting. I had been coaching gymnastics at a local private school, when I was introduced to their fencing master; the late Professor Jim Perry. He was genuinely a one-in-a-million coach, and clearly a world-class educator. Jim and I shared the same sports hall, and through many conversations, mini impromptu lessons (when we probably should have been working!), and me joining of several of his fencing clubs in Somerset, I learned more about life and principles of combat / motion in a few years, than I had in my whole life up to that point. With hindsight, I can say he naturally became my mentor. He exuded competence. I was not surprised to discover after a few years that his background was with the Special Forces, he had a CV the length of your arm! I could show him ideas from Kenpo - or wherever - and in turn, in a positive, empowering way, he would then explain to me how to improve it, in terms of brutal simple efficiency.

If there's one lesson I learned from him, it is the importance of relaxation. He pointed out to me that due to my over-conscientious nature and perfectionism, I was self-sabotaging and - in his words - the tension in my mind was spreading into my shoulders, arms and movements. He taught me that in a pressured or dangerous situation, you have to be able to (paradoxically) relax and trust your instincts, otherwise you probably won't react fast and effectively enough. A useful lesson. Furthermore, I have found in times of conflict, the ability to appear absolutely, almost abnormally calm can be a great diffuser of situations when dealing with aggression and confrontation. Not always of course, nor indeed for everyone, but often for me it has been the case.

Other words of wisdom he instilled were that whatever you do, you simply have to believe in it and your ability to implement it. Or otherwise change it. You can get yourself injured or killed through a bad choice in training or in reality; but to do so as a result of blindly following any instructor, system, or idea (all because you didn't / couldn't question the material and assumed it would work for you) is, in my mind, far worse. It's about taking absolute responsibility for yourself, and having the courage to go with your instincts about what is right for you, and to accept or embrace the consequences. Jim always did this, and was the ultimate maverick, and role model for this concept. He was totally happy for me to listen to his view, and challenge it, or even ignore it for that very reason. Direct, but respectful and mindful questions and answers are the way forward.

One thing I do now, is to treat every technique / scenario in training as a totally unique event. If I have to show a fixed 'book' technique, it is purely as a starting point, and I encourage improvisation, and then as the student progresses, and we see what their natural ability is, we guide them where necessary. Why? Because, in my view, adaptation and improvisation is the name of the game in self-defence, supported by strong psychological intent and conviction, of course. It's always a good thing to play devil's advocate with all training; it's safer to believe that anything we know might not work, and actively look for the glitches, and assume that for every move / technique there is a potential counter, and for every counter, there is another, and so on. I encourage my students and training partners to think like this, as no physical method, art, technique etc., is sacred, or above scrutiny when we're talking about people's safety. As long as the rapport and respect between everyone is there, and there is a positive learning atmosphere; challenging and even tearing apart ideas, and rebuilding them is real learning, and vital for progress. This is real education!

The crux of all learning is communication and, in my view, this is the paramount ability of any educator. You can have the best skill-set, the highest ranks, the most trophies, the most years of putting skills into practice, but if your communication skills and level of empathy and sensitivity to each student's needs aren't good enough, their learning will always be stifled. As an instructor, this delivery system for your 'product' of skills, guidance and knowledge is absolutely crucial.

I now believe that in the end, whatever system, art, method, (or none in particular) you choose, the most important question is: *Can I achieve what I set out to do with it?* And as a coach: *Can I ensure as far as possible that the student is genuinely empowered by my teaching, to the designated purpose?* This can be subjective, and often the root of bad politics between clubs and instructors. My belief is that if we have time to scrutinise and denigrate other instructors / practitioners, we should be using that time to address our own faults and weaknesses. I have yet to meet an instructor or practitioner who has no insecurities and demons. If such things inspire a positive path though, and drive us to improve personally, while maintaining professional integrity, then great. But more often than not, insecurity, in my experience is the main underlying cause of bad politics, and bad coaching.

As an instructor, I try to remain mindful of the fact that everyone is learning, (coach and student alike) with more to improve, and refinements to make. I believe that almost any system - or even any student - can still teach me something, perhaps not consciously or intentionally, and it's definitely true that the very act of teaching can give a different perspective and insight into the material. Whenever possible I always like to get the opinions of professional soldiers, doormen, fighters, police etc., on what has worked for them, and learn from the feedback of every student.

In terms of practical training methods, I choose them according to the individual student's needs; i.e. what they're training for, and their time commitment. Everyone needs good basic skills, good structure and form to function effectively. At a physical level, we train the basics of strikes, blocks, parries, kicks, chokes, escapes, grips, gouges, strangles, joint manipulations, throws / takedowns and falls etc., but chiefly, the underlying principles that make them work, and from different positions, and how to combine them effectively against vital targets. A good curriculum includes the five T's: *Techniques, Tactics, Targets, Timing* And *Training.* We also do the same incorporating weapons, mainly blades and sticks of varying sizes, depending on the purpose.

It's a popular cliché in what we all do nowadays, but 'simplicity and practicality' is the focus. In terms of designing and creating anything, we have the two qualities: *Form vs Function*. I tend to start people off learning what is most functional, then, if needs be, the more expressive, artistic *Form* can be practised. However, in simple terms, all students need to know the difference between what is a) scientifically effective in terms of surviving modern world violence, and b) more for show. Above all, understanding the limits, purpose, strengths and weaknesses of everything they do.

Nowadays, our students have the opportunity of regular cross-training in various systems including Muay Thai, boxing, kickboxing,

BJJ and grappling, Kenpo, and specific self-defence, with several instructors of diverse backgrounds. At the very least, studying other systems and cherry-picking useful elements, which is critical for creating a well-rounded technical skill-set. Pressure-testing is also vitally important, though of course the balance between safety and realism in training is a delicate one. Over the years I have taught specialist practical skills to everyone ranging from fighters, students, and the over 55s, to animal welfare professionals and victims of assaults.

General Philosophies for Coaching, Refinement and Improvement.

- One to one tuition is often the fastest way to learn anything.
- Quality is always better than quantity; practise and repetition is vital for progress, but can also be a great for creating and nurturing bad habits.
- The material has to be flexible to adjust for the recipient's needs!
- Economy of motion is imperative.
- Practise non-telegraphic movements, and train ways of naturally deceiving and hiding your intentions.
- Try and move smoothly, rather than just quickly, it's often faster, and generally more powerful.
- Use the path of least resistance
- Where possible either try to make everything you do, as 'subtle' as you can; effectively starving your opponent's senses of information, or conversely, just overwhelm them if that is your style / personality.
- Sometimes self-teaching, with the support of a good, secure coach, is the best way. Intuition is an extremely powerful force in learning.

Finally, this is one catalyst of forward thinking and harnessing initiative; when it comes to tradition and established thinking, sometimes it's better to break the rules, or never know them in the first place.

In the end though... do what works best for you!

*****

I would like to dedicate this in memory of my mentor, colleague, and friend Professor James 'Jim' Perry, 1946-2012; whose wisdom, support and generosity remains a great example and inspiration for all that we do.W: www.jimsworld.org

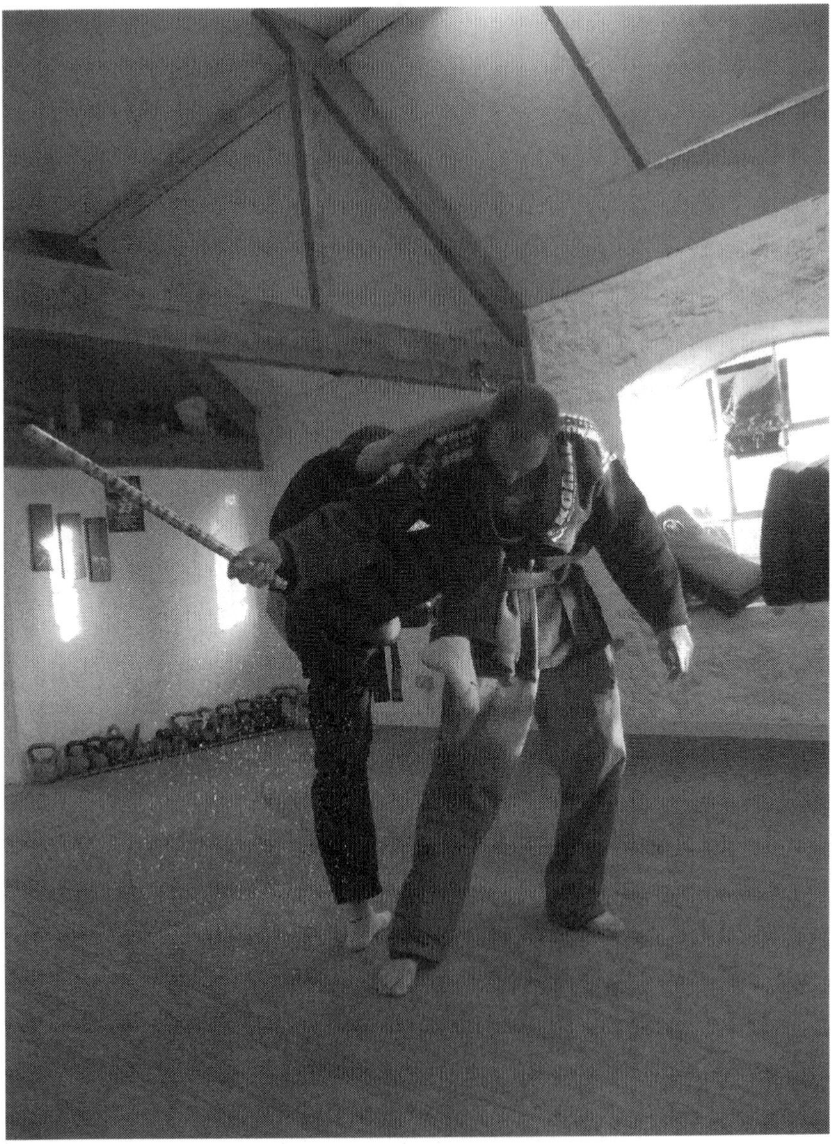

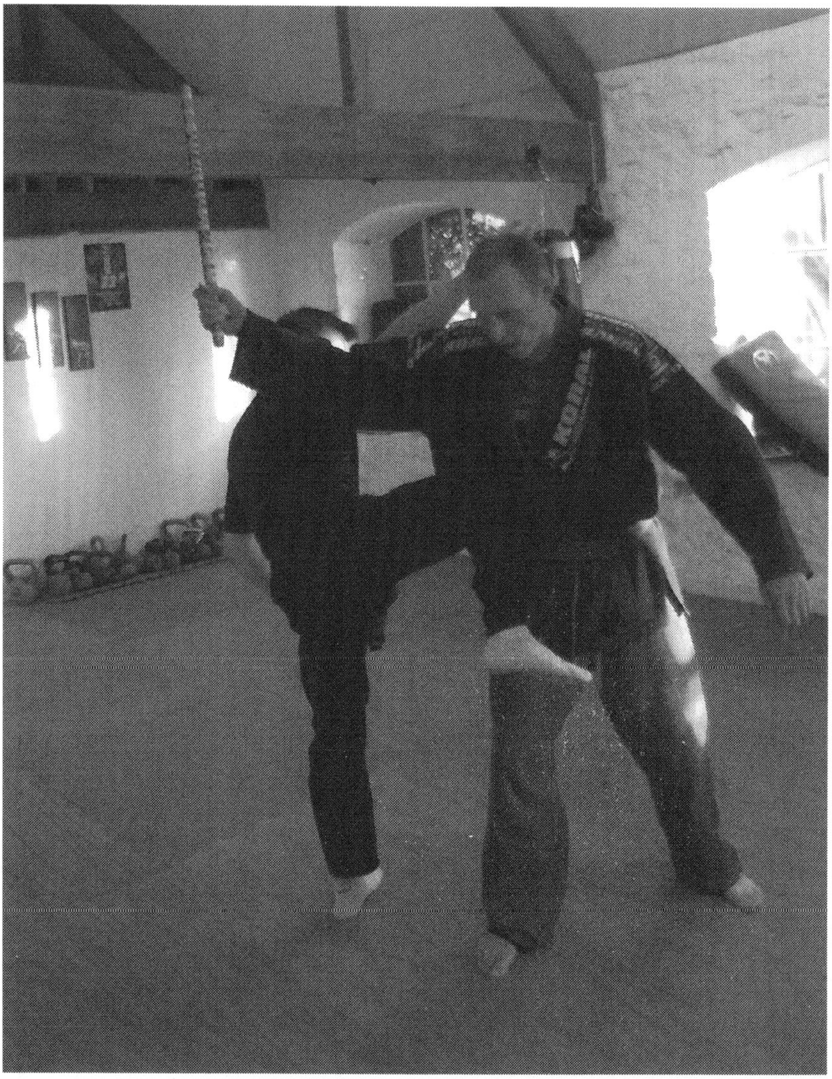

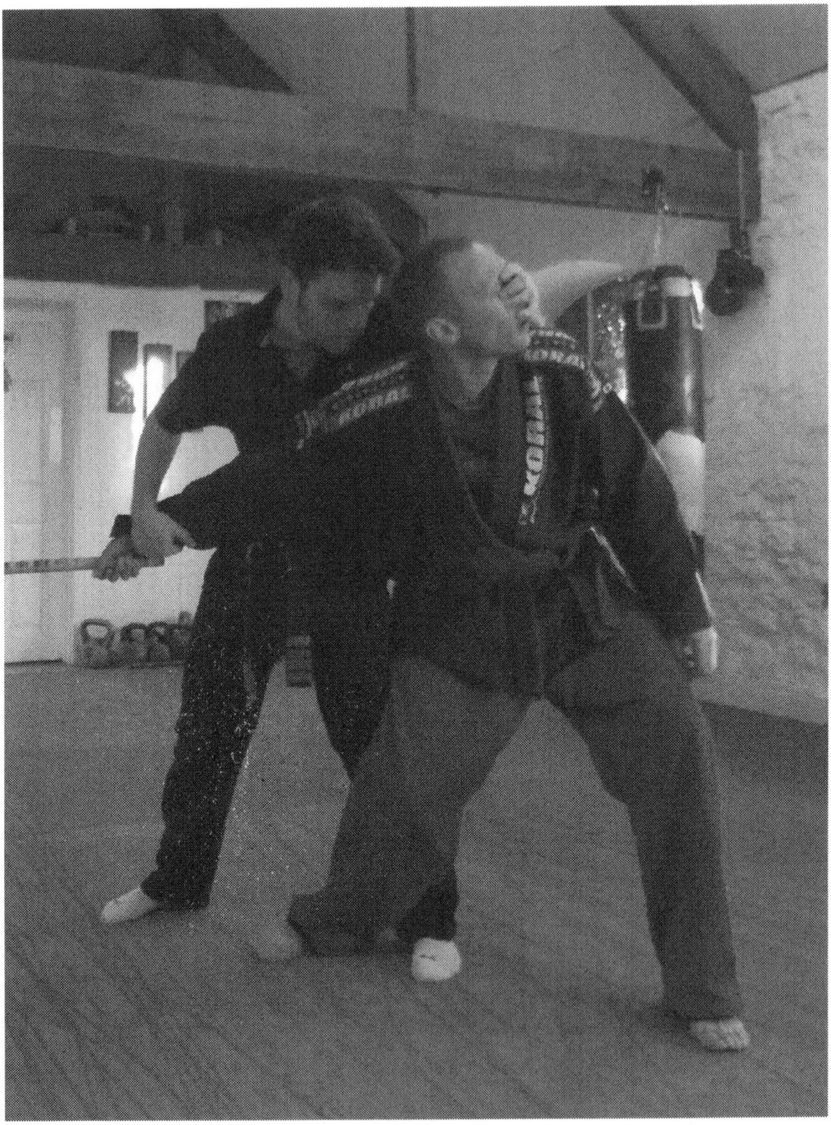

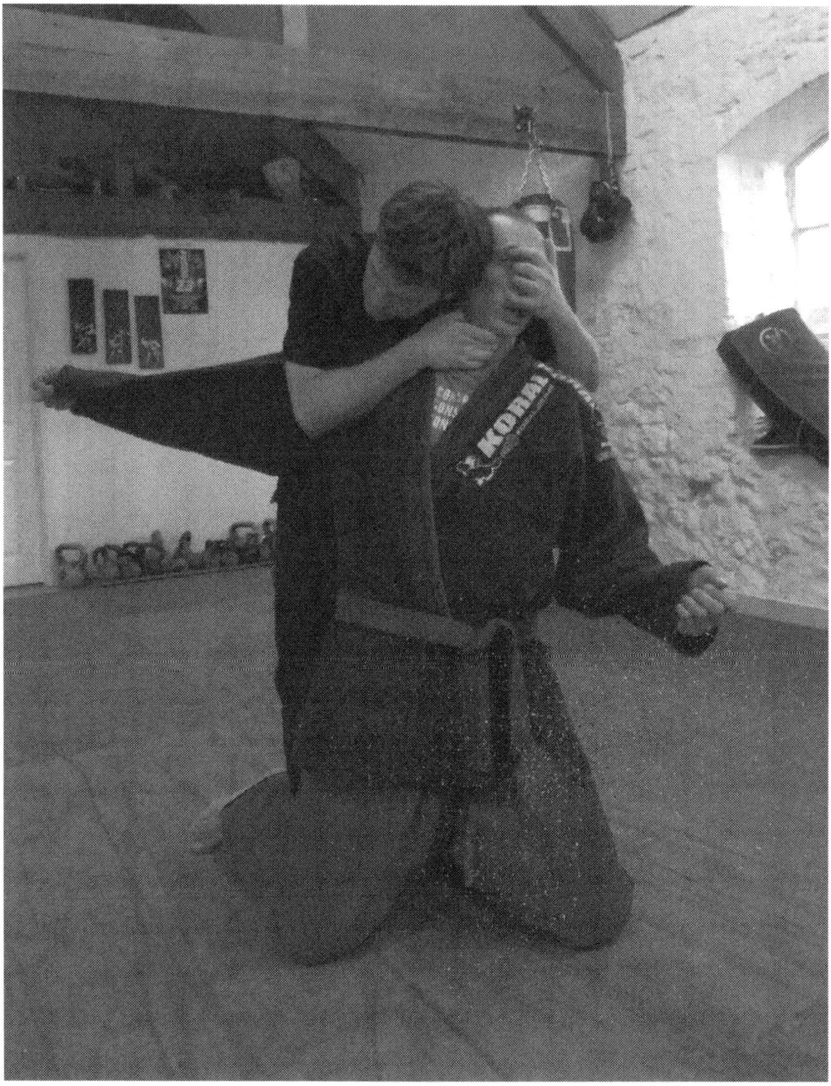

REAL COMBAT SYSTEM (The) – An Efficient and Tough Fighting System
By Tony Somers

The Real Combat System was started in Coventry in the 1990s by well known nightclub doorman Geoff Thompson. Coventry's claim to fame at the time was that, for its size, it was one of the most violent cities in Europe. Geoff ran a Shotokan karate club and was an excellent instructor, but he realised very early on that in the violent world of a nightclub door, the techniques in Shotokan were limited. Realising that in the real-life arena, where losing a fight could mean a hospital bed or even death, those who went first were usually victorious, and so he adapted his training to include a lot of Western boxing and pre-emption techniques. It's important to remember that these were the times before MMA was even heard of in this country. Geoff realised that it was fine to practice these techniques in a dojo or ring, but in a fight outside a nightclub or chip shop, how could you be sure that these techniques would work? So he came up with a concept (which travelled the world) called *Animal Day*, which some people say was the precursor to present day MMA.

Animal Days at his club were scary affairs; they consisted of all the club's members forming a circle, then two volunteers would stand in the centre of the circle and on Geoff's command, they would go for each other using whatever techniques they liked. It was quickly realised that in the majority of fights, if they went longer than a few seconds, they usually ended up in grappling range and so, to get competent at this range, a lot of us - including Geoff - started training in judo and free-style wrestling. Geoff taught techniques such as face bars, knee locks, ankle locks and many other very painful but effective techniques. Add in the pressure-testing aspects (Animal Days) to see which techniques really worked under pressure, and you've got a very efficient and very tough fighting system. Also, a big part of this training was to help practitioners handle their emotions under pressure, mainly fear and adrenalin - unless you work in an environment in which you experience fear and adrenalin on a regular basis, these emotions can cripple the best of fighters.

At that time we were also lucky enough to meet and train with Rick Young who was a regular visitor to Brazil and who was one of only a handful of Westerners to have a black belt in BJJ under Mauricio

Gomes (Maurício Motta Gomes is a practitioner of Brazilian Ju-jitsu, one of the six people to have been promoted to black belt by the famous Rolls Gracie prior to Gracie's untimely death. He has been training and teaching Brazilian Ju-jitsu for over fifty years and at present holds the rank of 7th degree black and red belt), as well as people such as Neil Adams in judo, Peter Conserdine kick-boxing and self protection expert, and Dave Turton's Combat Ju-jitsu, as well as several professional boxing coaches. It's important to remember that it was very unusual to have this type of all round training in the martial arts world at this time.

Geoff eventually moved into the world of writing and films and left the Real Combat System in the hands of Matty Evans and myself. Matty Evans is 6th dan Real Combat System, two times British champion Vale Tudo. 1st dan Combat Ju-jitsu under Dave Turton, 1st dan Shotokan karate, as well as freestyle Greco Roman wrestling coach and NVQ level 3 Personal Trainer and my Joint Chief Instructor.

The system is mainly about street self-defence and as such now includes a lot of aspects surrounding conflict management. We teach awareness skills, posturing and effective communications skills (to avoid verbal conflict), attack rituals and aspects of the law surrounding self-defence. We also put a lot of emphasis on understanding and controlling fear, covering areas such as adrenal maps and sharing real-life experiences - the world has changed and is still changing rapidly and therefore our biggest emphasis is on avoiding conflict and focusing on pre-emption in a physical confrontation; this is the jewel in our crown.

I do a lot of work as a counsellor, working in areas such as bereavement, self-worth, depression and anxiety, and have found that helping to also build self-confidence through training helps people to deal more effectively with the everyday pressures of life. We do our best to lead by example and don't bad-mouth anyone or any other system, and we do our very best to motivate and build confidence in everyone we meet.

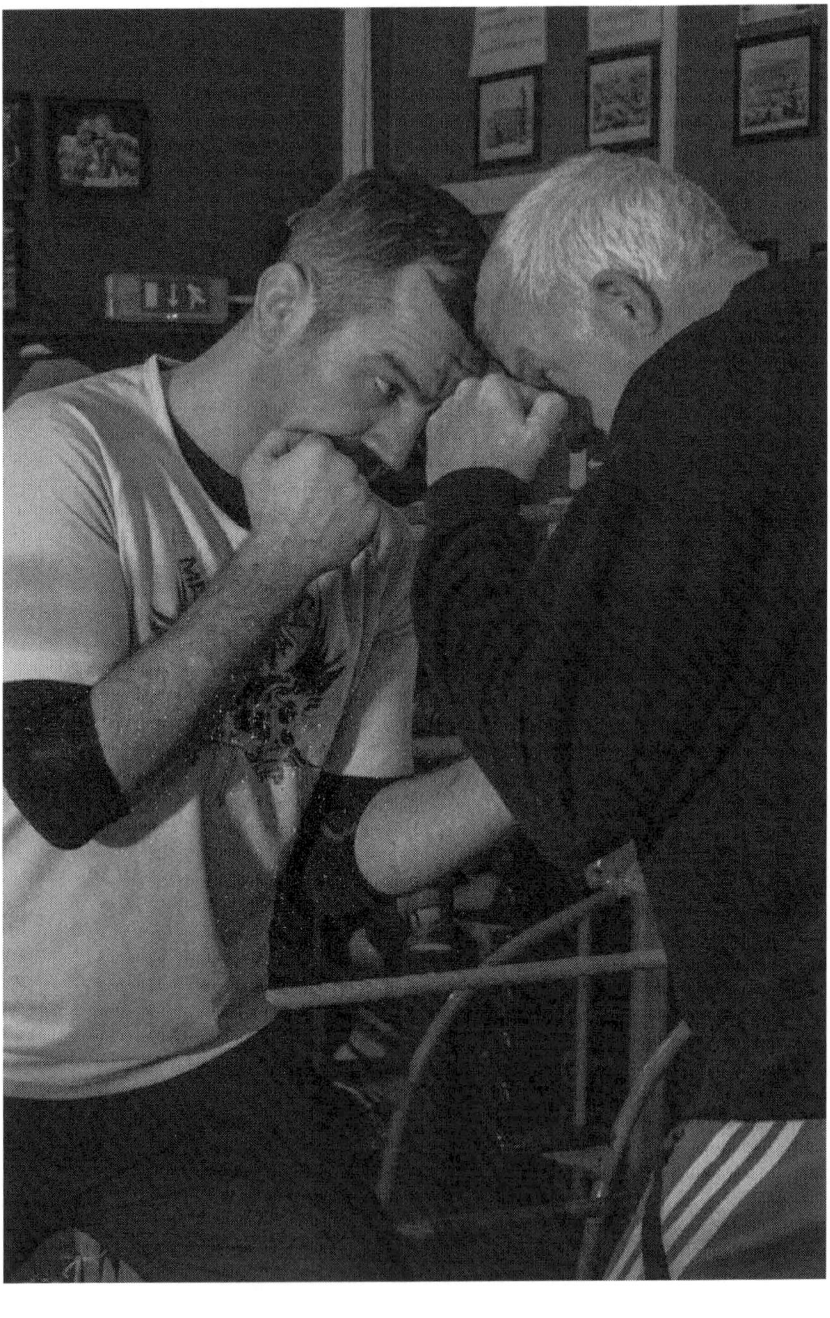

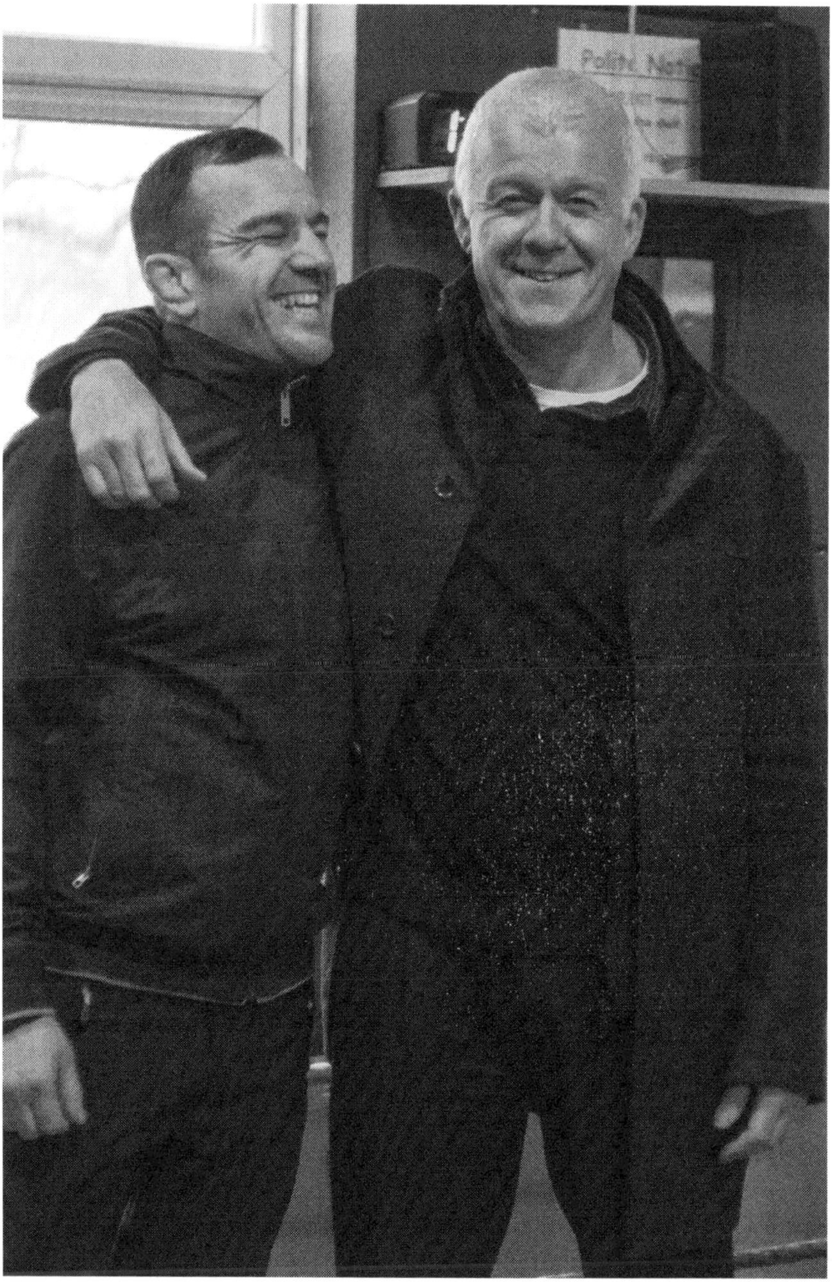

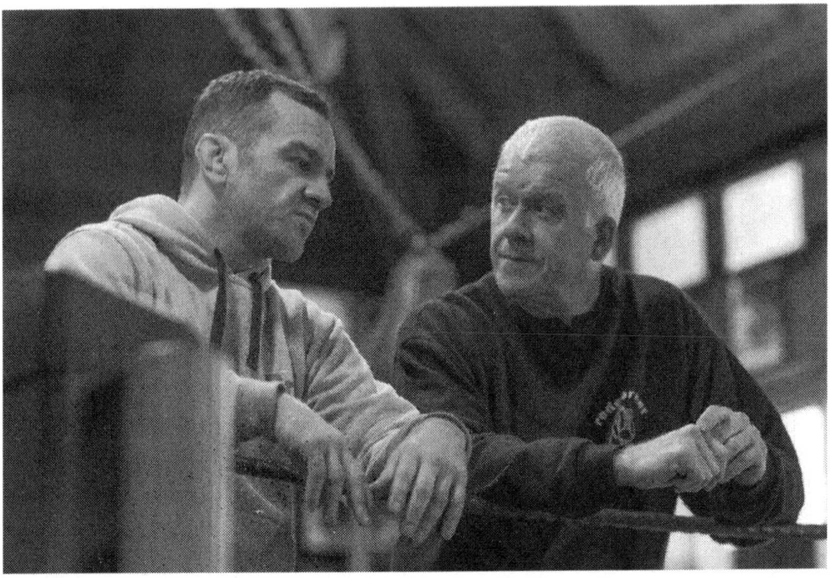

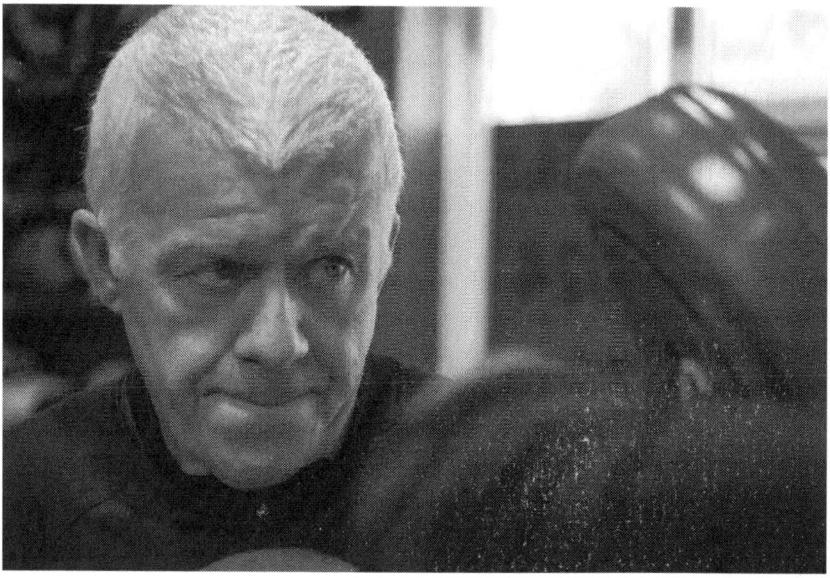

SPHERE COMBAT SYSTEM - Based Around Natural Responses to Action Under Stress

By Peter Ellis

Sphere Combat Systems is an intensive close quarter combat system utilised by Special Force units and bodyguards around the world, and is based around *natural* responses to action under stress conditions, and not on attempts to change natural reactions to sudden or instant action. This state of conditioning can only be achieved in the way that you train or practice for these conditions. The reality is that if you were compromised and have to react to an instant burst of movement in the form of an immediate aggressive action, you will almost certainly react in one of the following manners; you will either flinch making yourself less of a target, or you will flinch and leap away from the point of aggression. A good example of this is when an explosion occurs, there is a flinch, leap and probably fall to the ground.

I have assessed and evaluated countless combatants during training and in real-life situations, who tend to expend themselves from the outset and, when faced with a formidable opponent, find themselves having to deal with extreme fatigue after a short time.

The tactically correct combatant must remain in a state of readiness before any encounter, and must be able to achieve the objective with controlled aggression, but must also be able to switch off the controlled aggression after the encounter, returning to a state of readiness or non-tactical demeanour. It could be stress-related, or a lack of concentration, or even laziness, or all three, or possibly not being ready psychologically and physically in control.

The reality is simple; train and practice the combative way where you presume you will get wounded, injured, fatigued, dehydrated or with an aggressor who is going to kill you, and in this way you will stand a lot better chance in combat.

To understand the body's reactions to a conflict situation, or being attacked, can be summed up in several ways; interpersonal human aggression creates a toxic atmosphere in warriors everywhere. Our bodies will respond in ways that we may not be able to control but must understand nonetheless if we are to competently handle a lethal threat. Automatic systems designed for thoughtless survival kick in to gear, adrenaline is released, digestive processes cease and even bladder and sphincter control is lost. The reason for bringing this information to your attention is to emphasise the importance of realistic pressurised and stressful training which can create an instinctive response to a deadly threat. It makes no difference if you know one move, or thousands; you can never predict when you will be attacked. Training for a specific response to a specific attack, and your self-protection will fail, as an attack in progress becomes dynamic and will change in an instant, and will keep on changing until you are seriously injured or dead. Believing that one 'magic' technique will work against a hundred different attacks is suicidal. It is far better to develop the ability to improvise and adapt any strike, or hold from any position spontaneously with power, accuracy and balance. Sphere Combat is a combination of improvisation, survival and escape, and not fancy acrobatic moves or sport fighting in the ring with a referee present.

Sphere Combat Systems is popular with international Special Forces units, but also with close protection operators and companies around the world. Although a close protection operative's role isn't about confrontation escalation, operatives must be able to handle any form of confrontation including - in the worst case scenario – physical confrontation and therefore Sphere Combat offers tactics and strategies to implement in these situations. Sphere Combat is also taught to the general public as it can be modified and developed to suit just about everyone, which many other martial art and combat systems cannot. Progression is always on-going in the system.

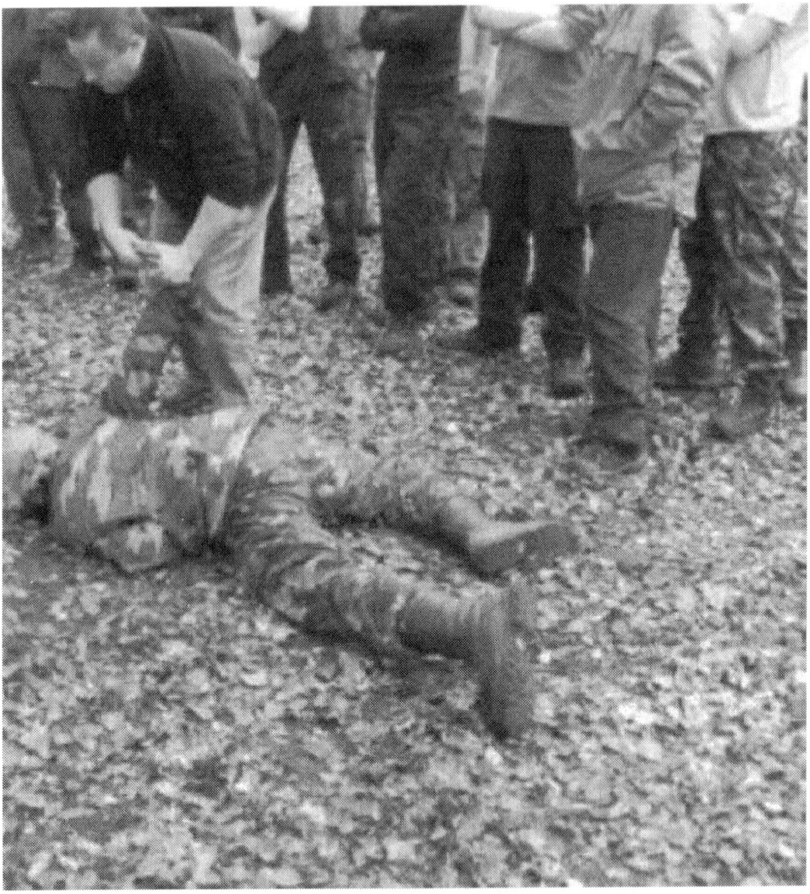

STAGE COMBAT - From Karado to Kong

By Cynthia Morrison.

Not so long ago an acquaintance asked me what I would recommend for their children that would assist in directing them towards a positive attitude in life. She was concerned about keeping them on the straight and narrow. I immediately suggested martial art classes. She wondered why so? I explained to her that this activity would teach them not only self-defence, discipline and focus, but respect for others as well.

There were two factors that initially led me to martial arts. The first was a Hollywood production of *Kung Fu,* an American television series presenting actor David Carradine as Caine. Being in my teenage years, I was impressed by Caine's ability to master almost any situation by using his philosophies or martial art skill. The second inspirational element was my purple Western flyer bicycle that I was riding down 14th Court when I witnessed a neighbour and his brother practising body throws in their front-yard. I immediately applied the brakes and asked where they had learned their manoeuvrers. They invited me to class with them and I excitedly went along!

When I arrived to the dojo where class was held, I didn't find Caine but I did find Karado karate. This martial art style was developed by Grand Master Warren Siciliano, who was bodyguard to Presidents Roosevelt, Truman, Eisenhower, Kennedy and Nixon. Karado is an eclectic mixture of Goju-Ryu, Isshinryu, Tae Kwon Do and kung fu. I spent a number of the following years dedicated to a combination of both learning and teaching this wonderful defensive art.

Theatrical Conflict

Long after my purple bicycle was inherited at the hands of my cousin Mary, I was reaching achievement with a transitional period of mounted combat at international jousting tournaments. Part of this training system was technique with sword, both on horse and on foot. This activity offered authentic competition in the sport of jousting, as well as displays at festivals. The displays of course included theatrical effects. To hone my acting skills I joined a local acting school led by American film icon Burt Reynolds.

Having taught specialised combat skills to my jousting club members over a five year span, this inspired me to share 'mock combat' with fellow actors. Stage combat is a specialised technique in theatre designed to create the illusion of physical combat without causing harm to the performers. Safety should be a fight director's first and foremost concern.

One of the most memorable moments with regard to stage combat was during those years of study with Mr. Reynolds. I was in rehearsal for a showcase scene that he had assigned to me. I played a suicidal and crazed individual who was attempting to provoke an elder woman into a physical altercation. Mr. Reynolds entered the stage to direct the actress in her part, and had her sit on the sidelines to observe him. The scene required that I convince my scene partner to pick up a switch-blade that I had thrown to the ground. There we were, locked into each other's eyes as I aggressively and verbally demanded that he challenge me with the knife. Then, all of the sudden, I fell into something that actors should avoid; I briefly went 'out of character' as I met the realization that there I was actually in a mock knife-fighting scene with Navajo Joe, the American Indian protagonist that Reynolds played in a film by the same name when I was seven years old. That moment, for me, could only define; *Awe-inspiring*.

Sticks And Stones

Victorian self-defence techniques including use of walking canes and attire came into play for theatrical purpose inspired by my personal study of Bartitsu (see article by Adam Parsons in this book). Altercations in film were suddenly recognized in a different light. A great example of these methods can be found in the 1946 production of *Terror by Night* featuring actor Basil Rathbone as the famous detective Sherlock Holmes created by Sir Arthur Conan Doyle. The story includes Holmes' journey on a train where he encounters a jewel thief. The take down of the suspect becomes a mystery in itself as Holmes intentionally apprehends the 'falsely accused,' only to bring forth and reveal the genuine criminal. The struggle between Holmes and his first arrest found the suspect on the floor confined between the narrow seating rows of the train as Holmes peeled his opponent's trench coat from his body. Holmes then wrapped the coat around the man in order to constrict his movement as he delivered the suspect to a police constable.

Hollywood and the development of motion pictures have given new meaning to surviving physical threat by unconventional means of defence. The most recent presentation of combative entertainment can be witnessed in the newly released *KONG: Skull Island* (2017). Not only does this film rank high with its monstrous characters, but also with its combative scenarios. Displays of skilful pool cue application as the protagonist defeats three perpetrators in a matter of seconds by meticulous choreography during a billiards game. Even more impressive are some of the techniques utilized by KONG himself. Just imagine an enormous towering primate ripping a tree from the earth and using one hand to drag it through the other hand in order to clear the branches from its trunk then swinging it in the manner of a baseball bat against his screaming monstrous dragon-type antagonist. This production is a must see for anyone seeking an excellent thriller!

Another aspect that I immediately appreciated about KONG is the fact that the director defines KONG as the 'animal' and not so much as 'the monster.' One detail that hit home with me is when KONG beats his chest, as is the gorilla's nature. This primate gesture is shared within my award winning novelette *Adelia of the Coliseum* which is a story of an ancient Gladitrix of Rome. In a scene from the book, Rekanna, a retired gladiatrix, shares her experienced knowledge with Adelia about gorilla's and their power located in the area known as the soloplex.

"...You know the big apes they bring from the south?" (for the gladiator games)

"Yes Rekanna."

"You remember ever seeing them beat their chests with their fists?"

"Yes! I do."

"The ape does not do this to look funny. He is building his strength to fight. He gives a warning of how strong he is. He prepares for battle. Animals are many times smarter than us. In this case you see why."

I'm sure that movie theatre patrons watching *KONG: Skull Island* would agree with Rekanna's opinion.

Food Fight Anyone?

Although I am a fan of film making slapstick comedy, I'm not referring to the pie-in-the-face type food fight. Part of my stage combat curriculum includes the use of grapes. How could food items as menial as grapes be of any benefit during the heat of battle you may ask? Perhaps you'll grasp my meaning the next time a watering sprinkler surprisingly hits the wind-shield of your moving vehicle unexpectedly. The natural reflex of blinking eyes takes one third of a second of time. Let's compare that to the record punching time of Ian Bishop in the United Kingdom. Ian's punching record consists of nineteen punches executed within one second time. Nineteen divided by three, or one third, is six point three (6.3) punches in a third of a second. Mind you, he holds a world record for it. So let's assume that a typical opponent could perform in half his time. This would bring us to three punches within one third of a second. Can a few grapes flung into an opponent's face create a slight advantage? Of course! Not only that, but the event makes a theatrical presentation simply just that more entertaining. Now if they can only create grapes on a scale for KONG!

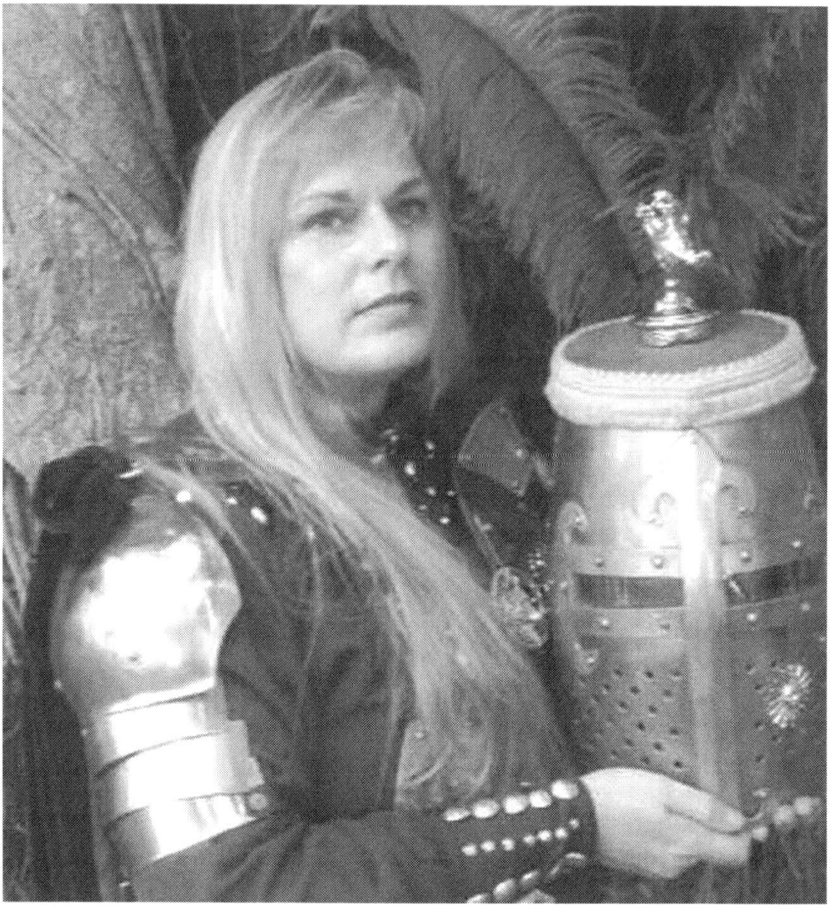

TOTAL KRAV MAGA - A Dynamic and Practical Combat System

By Nick Maison - UK

Krav Maga is a reality based self-defence and combat system. Some martial arts are sport based, while others may be based on tradition or culture. Krav Maga is very much a dynamic and practical system dealing with current 'issues of the day' when it comes to assault or aggressive behaviour.

Imagine this... It's 22:00, you're tired and walking towards your car, heading home after the gym. The multi-storey car park is desolate, except for the screech of some tyres on the level below. As you approach your car, in the window you see the reflection of two people behind you. You turn around and one gestures a knife at you and whispers "car keys... now!"

Krav Maga teaches you how to deal with the stress of these kinds of situations and to act quickly with an appropriate solution. You could respond 'pre-fight', meaning do something pre-emptive or preventative whilst still in the threat stage. You could also respond during the 'fight', meaning defending a 'dynamic' attack, neutralise the threat and escape. Follow up action is considered the 'post-fight.' Post-fight we check ourselves for injuries, personal belongings and try to build up an image of the attacker(s), so we can inform the appropriate authorities and provide a description.

Krav Maga is about teaching people to defend themselves against very real problems in today's unpredictable society. I don't consider the system to be a martial art; there are no *artistic* elements to it; no forms, no katas no competitive events. It is just a system which offers solutions to problems which can be life-threatening. In other styles of martial arts, the practitioner can be tested by gradings, tournaments, patterns, forms and katas. In Krav Maga we test our practitioners by trying to recreate realistic scenarios in simulations and drills. We train systematically to a fixed syllabus, but every so often, we take our training out of the gym and put ourselves in a real environment, whether it be training in low light, in and around our cars, hiring an aircraft or train carriage for a workshop, or training at night in a cold and wet park.

However, Krav Maga still uses many elements associated with sports or regular fighting systems; we have energetic warm-ups, we stretch and develop our bodies and minds with exercise and training drills, but we do not focus on competitions or tournaments because in real life there is no ideal fighting arena, such as a ring or matted floor. There will be no referee to stop the fight if it looks like one person is sustaining injuries, and there is no time limit. In reality you are likely to face more than one attacker, they will probably be armed, whether that is with a purposely designed weapon like a knife or gun, or it is an improvised weapon like a glass they snatched off a table. They will not necessarily be in your weight category, and you will in most cases not be mentally prepared or have the time to perform some kind of physical preparation or warm up.

There has been a huge increase in interest about Krav Maga over the past eight years and you can now find many different organisations offering various styles of Krav Maga, operating in almost every city and country around the world.

Krav Maga is actually Hebrew for 'contact fight' and was developed as a system of self-defence by the late Imi Lichtenfeld. In 1948, when Israel was formed and the Israeli Defence Force (IDF) was created, Imi was the head of the IDF physical training branch and developed the system as the force's hand-to-hand combat system. When Imi retired in 1964, he developed Krav Maga further as a self-defence system for civilians, opening his first club in Netanya, Israel. In the early '90s, Krav Maga left the borders of Israel and Imi's longest and most dedicated student, Eyal Yanilov took it upon himself to spread the word of Krav Maga in Europe and the USA.

As Krav Maga grew in popularity there became a need for some kind of organisation and in 1996 the International Krav Maga Federation (IKMF) was born lead by Eyal. The IKMF was then developed into Krav Maga Global (KMG) around 2010 and Eyal Yanilov continues to develop the system and educate his Global & International Training Team along with instructors and students all over the world in over sixty countries.

Krav Maga Global operate a well-structured training system for various self-defence requirements. In many countries in Eastern Europe and South America, the Police and Military units train in Krav Maga under Krav Maga Global (KMG). There are specific courses and techniques for military operatives involving work with firearms, disarming of long weapons and tactical behaviour for particular job roles. The same can be said for law enforcement or anti-terrorist operatives, executive or close protection operatives, and of course self-defence for civilians.

Krav Maga Global have run courses for police forces in many Western European countries and the USA. The Metropolitan Police and various other UK constabularies have also trained under KMG, however the civilian Krav Maga branch is where most people in the UK will get access to Krav Maga, via a registered club.

Today, we believe the attraction to Krav Maga is about the simplicity it offers. It is easy to learn, effective and achieves higher levels of physically fitness, and also makes the participants more mentally aware. Many students comment on how much more confident they feel.

The world is becoming a dangerous place and criminals are willing to take more risks and commit more serious crimes without care for the consequences. As normal members of society we are, by law, allowed to defend ourselves against violence and crime. People know this and are looking for a way to protect their loved ones, themselves and their property, particularly with the recent wave of terrorism and knife crime in the UK over the past ten years.

The reality based training offered within Krav Maga seems to be ticking the boxes for people who may not want the tradition and protocol of martial arts, or who may be intimidated by the fierce image of the 'cage' in MMA, or other competitive martial arts. In a sentence; *"Krav Maga can be practised by anyone, any age and any level of fitness."* It appeals to a broad spectrum of society who just want to feel safe on the streets of their town or at home.

So, imagine this. It's 22.00, you're tired and walking towards your car, heading home after the gym. The multi-storey car park is desolate, except for screech of some tyres on the level below. As you approach your car, in the driver's window you see the reflection of two people behind you. You turn around and one gestures a knife at you and whispers "car keys... now!" You turn around and look at the two young men in front of you wearing hoodies... You say: "Look guys... back off!" The guy with the knife raises his hand holding the knife towards you. Before he can get close enough, you use your gym bag as a shield and deliver a kick to the groin. He's on his knees, and you move out of the line of attack and hit him again with bag. The knife drops from his hands and you kick it under your car. The second guy attempts to grab you by the collar then punch you. You simultaneously block his punch and counter-attack him with another punch, followed by knee to the groin and hammer punch the back of his head. You move out his line of attack, scan the area for other attackers. The coast is clear so you get in your car, lock the doors and drive to safe place. You then take out your mobile and call the police. As you recover from the stress of the attempted mugging your thoughts become clear and you think to yourself: *'I'm glad tonight's Krav Maga lesson at the gym was about multiple attackers.'*

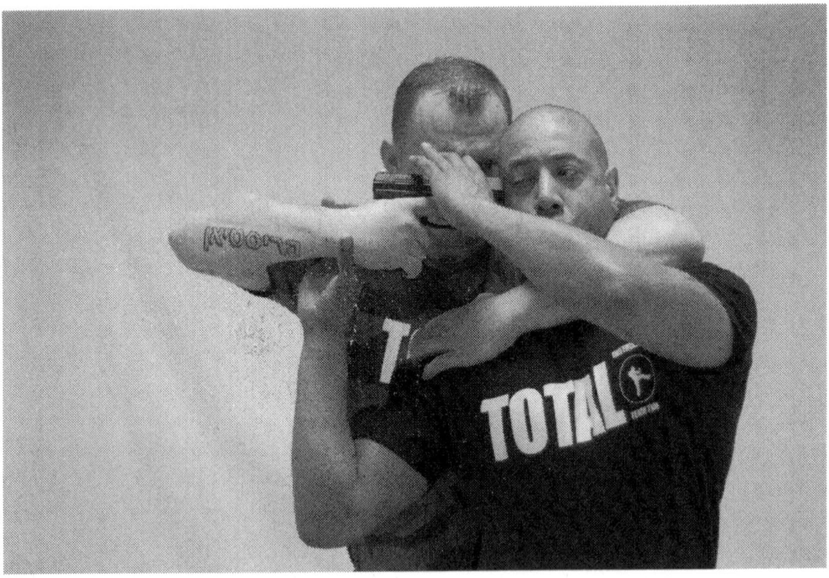
TOTAL

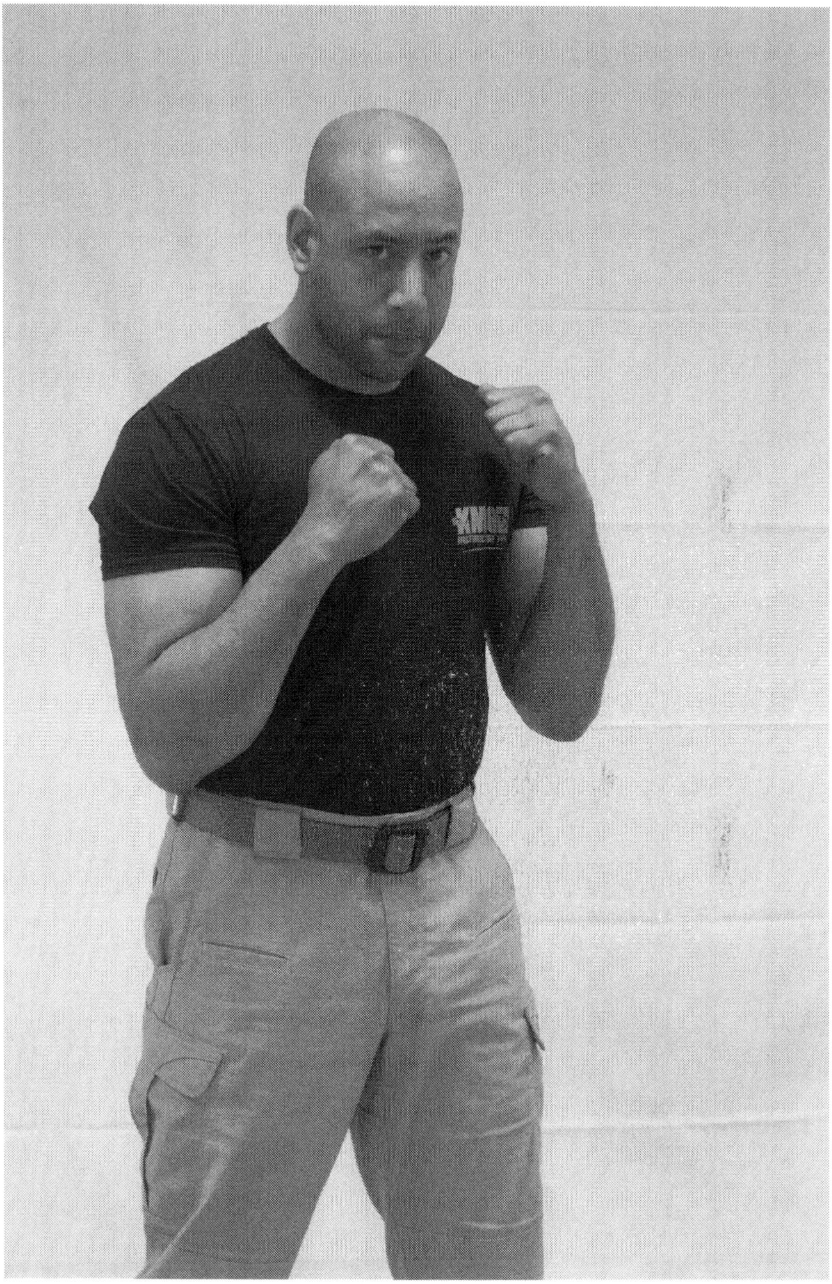

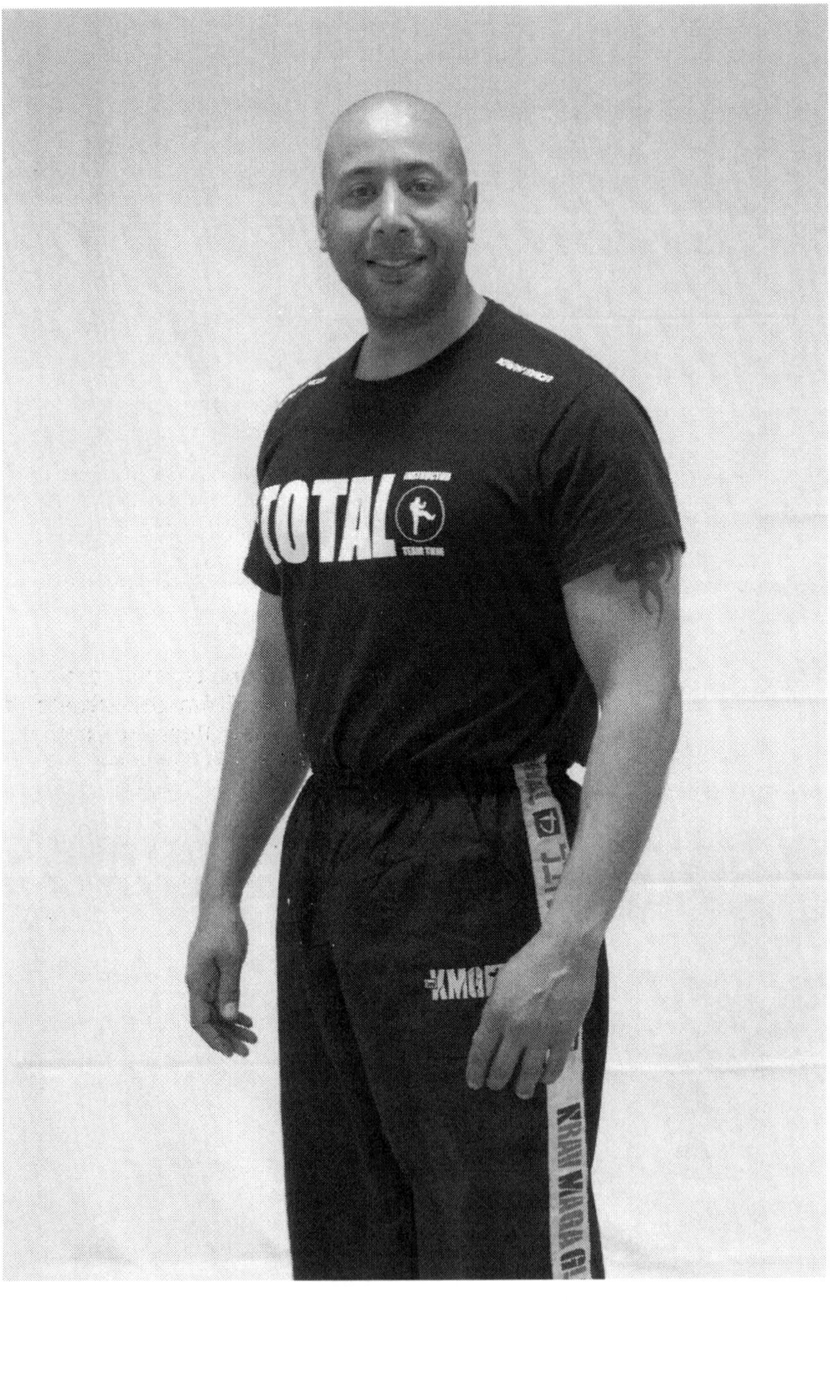
TOTAL
KMG
KRAV MAGA

V.I.P.A. TACTICAL TRAINING SYSTEM - Embracing Change, Evolvement and Open Mindedness

By Paul 'Rock' Higgins

The VIPA Tactical Training System is not a static system as is karate, kung fu or judo for example; by static I mean something that has not changed from its traditional roots over long periods of time, or something that has not kept up with modern threats and combat that is found in today's modern world. If the instructor is not teaching applications that belong on the street, or battlefield, then they are teaching a 'Do' a 'Way.' More often today; martial arts are a way to keep fit or for inner harmony, a way to overcome oneself and become a better person. These are more akin to a moving form of meditation and are great for those looking for the path that martial arts provide; and it is a fantastic path to tread. However having said that, they are not in any way combat systems which modern warriors require to win in whatever environment they may find themselves.

From its conception in the late '80s, VIPA has evolved and continues to evolve as threats and environments change. From the streets of Northern Ireland and training for combat against Russian Spetsnaz Special Forces, to the 1991 Gulf War, VIPA has adapted to its environments and continues to do so with Civilian Self Protection Programs, Police Defence Tactics and Close Protection Combat Systems alongside Military Close Quarter Combat.

VIPA as a combat system is as its name implies and either enhances or negates the effects that are involved in the Fight-Freeze-Flight model.

It is **V**iolent, it is **I**mmediate, it is **P**ositive, it is **A**ction!

VIPA embraces change, evolvement, open mindedness and, above all, the mind-set of being combat focused at all times.

VIPA is a *'Sphere of Influence'* and at the centre of the sphere are the *'Core Concepts'*; the basic vital skills that are required of any means of combat. There is nothing new in the skills of the Core Concepts, but what is different about VIPA's Core Concepts is how they are applied.

The Core Concepts (see illustration page 168) are a means to an end. The means are the strategies, tactics and the techniques. The end, well... that has many forms; is it to win the next time you are attacked? Is it not to get into a position where you are attacked ever again? Is to protect your loved ones or as a professional close protection operator is it to protect the life or lives of your Principal/s? As a law enforcement officer, is it to detain a suspect? Or as a soldier is it to win and stay alive on the battlefield? The only real 'End' is what you as an individual are training towards.

There are four specific areas of combat; Military Close Quarter Combat, Close Protection Combat Systems, Civilian Self-Protection Program, Police Defence Tactics. Each is its own discipline and each takes what it needs from the Core Concepts. Although VIPA is a complete system; not everything within the Core Concepts is suitable for each of the four specific areas of combat, as we all live and work in different actualities. Where you live and work, and the laws of the land, will dictate what skills you require to achieve your end goal. So, VIPA in one country for one person may be different to VIPA for another person in another country.

Here in the UK we are not allowed to carry knives or firearms for defensive purposes, therefore, there is no need to teach civilians knife fighting or gun fighting for combat. Edged weapon defence and firearm disarming techniques though are a different matter and are taught. VIPA in the USA has gun fighting as part of its Core Concepts for the Civilian Self Protection Program, but again that is only if that State allows for CCW or firearms for home defence. Similarly, what the soldier requires to win in combat on the battlefield is different to what the police officer requires to arrest someone on the street.

The Core Concepts hold the key to the VIPA system in its evolvement and diversity. The tactics and techniques employed by the soldier changes as the enemy changes, from fighting conventional troops with the same uniform, kit, weapons and in certain cases a dedicated close quarter combat system, to the terrorists dressed in local or mixtures of clothing and armed with an array of weaponry and with who-knows-what standard of close quarter combat skills. Adaptability is the mother of all skill-sets and one embraced by the VIPA system.

The Core Concepts being a Sphere of Influence, is a wheel that is constantly turning and, as such, each specific area of combat influences the others. The Close Protection Combat Systems have military influences within its PSD / hostile environments, and police arrest and restraint in the Residential Security Team role and some civilian options for the unarmed close protection operator.

The civilian has to deal with a myriad of threats on the streets and the threats will differ depending on the area or country of residence or the country being visited. The student of the VIPA system has to be constantly open to diversification as threats can change all too quickly.

Training for all four specific areas of combat would not be complete if only the physical aspects were taught; the VIPA system involves classroom learning with many lectures and academic studies including physiology, terrorist and criminal psychology, threat assessments, criminology, terrorism awareness, anti-terrorism awareness, force options, the law, aggression management & aggression continuum, home security, mobile security, to name but a few, making for an all-round system where knowledge and skill are combined and constantly updated to keep up with the ever changing threats posed by the various members of the criminal fraternity.

Core Concepts
1 overall doctrine 4 specific doctrines
4 specific areas of combat 1 complete system

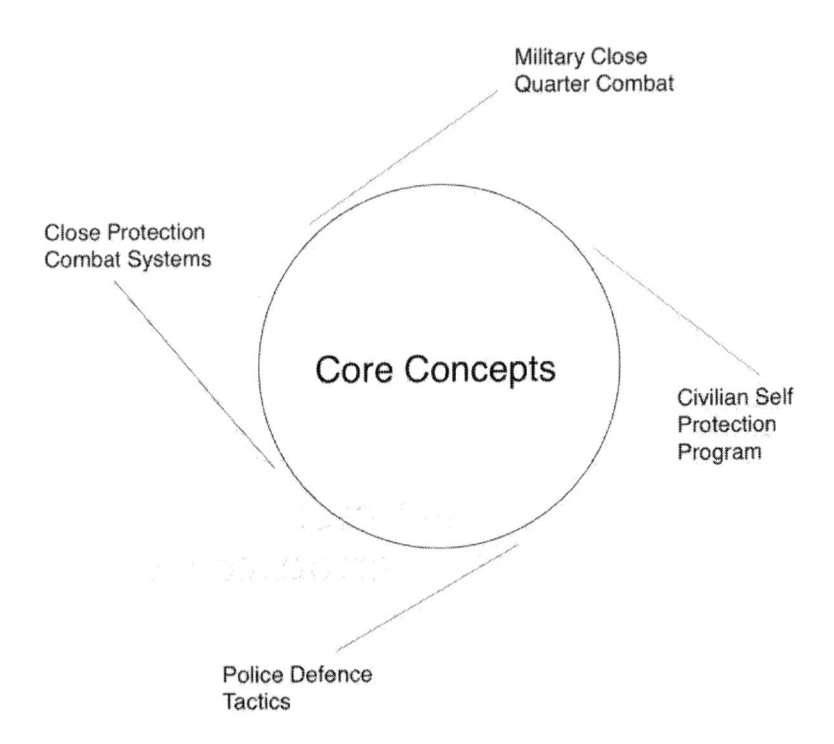

Military Close
Quarter Combat

Close Protection
Combat Systems

Core Concepts

Civilian Self
Protection
Program

Police Defence
Tactics

Fancy showcasing your system or style in *Volume 2 - More Urban Self-Defence and Close Quarter Combat Systems*?

Contact me:
Robin@RobinBarratt.co.uk

FINDING WORK AS A CLOSE PROTECTION SPECIALIST (BODYGUARD): 2015 - 16 Edition

By Robin Barratt

With ten new chapters including High Risk Close Protection, Executive Driving and making your CV more noticeable, from contributors including driver training professional Tony Scotti, former Royal Navy Commando and martial arts expert Tyrrel Francis, and private security contractor Richard Pendry, this is a vital manual for training and job hunting.

Updated for 2015 – 2016, with tens of thousands of people reading it worldwide, Finding Work as a Close Protection Specialist (Bodyguard) is the most widely read manual of its kind, ever! A must read for anyone thinking about entering the protection industry, or already qualified and looking for work.

"A must read and an essential weapon in your job search arsenal!" Contractor in Iraq

Paperback ISBN: 978-1515398325
Kindle ASIN: B013XG1MJU
FREE TO DOWNLOAD from www.RobinBarratt.co.uk

BRITAIN'S TOUGHEST WOMEN - Some of the Toughest Women Bodyguards, Bouncers, Bodybuilders, Boxers, Martial Artists and MMA Fighters in the UK
By Robin Barratt

Britain's Toughest Women spotlights some of the toughest female bodyguards, bouncers, bodybuilders, boxers, martial artists and MMA fighters in the UK; women who live, work or play in a tough world. Biography based chapters, looking at their past, present and plans for the future, what inspires and motivates them, and why they do what they do! For some it's having a tough, challenging or traumatic upbringing, or feeling an underachiever at home or at school, or being bullied, or abused, or being pushed into things by their friends or family, or just overcoming life's challenges. For others it's solely their mindset and attitude, or simply following their dreams. It can be all sorts of things, and each person has their own, unique and fascinating story. All the women featured here have chosen to be recognised for doing something exceptional and different; from working on the front-line in Iraq, to standing on stage as a competitive bodybuilder or entering the arena as an MMA fighter or boxer. This book not only aims to spotlight these incredible women, but aims to motivate and inspire others, and to show that whatever background you're from, and whatever life's challenges and difficulties you've had, you can achieve too.

Paperback ISBN: 978-1508941262
Kindle ASIN: B00WA7OT0S

DOOR GIRLS - Interviews With 25 Women About Their Life Working on the Doors of Clubs and Pubs Across the UK

By Robin Barratt

In this no-holds-barred book, women talk openly and honestly about their life working the doors of clubs and pubs across the UK and abroad.

A must read...!

AVAILABLE SUMMER 2017 AS PAPERBACK & KINDLE FROM AMAZON WEBSITES WORLDWIDE!

FANCY CONTRIBUTING?

If you're female and currently working the doors, or have spent a lot of time working the doors, and fancy being interviewed for this book, please contact me. I'll then try to get to meet you somewhere and spend a few hours over coffee chatting with you about your life working the doors. Alternatively I can send you questions via email for you to answer at your leisure. Email me at Robin@DoorGirls.co.uk

DEADLINE JULY 31st 2017

www.RobinBarratt.co.uk

Printed in Great Britain
by Amazon